REAL MONEY ANSWERS®
FOR
EVERY WOMAN

The Wisdom & Wealth Money Maven

PATRICE C. WASHINGTON

Presents

How to Win the Money Game with or without a Man!

What People Are Saying About . . .

PATRICE C. WASHINGTON
Author | Speaker | Coach

Patrice explains money with a practicality I have never EVER experienced before. She makes managing money fun and a journey you can look forward to. I never felt like I could achieve my financial goals, but today I'm 1000% more hopeful because of her words.

> Dominique M.
> Childcare Provider
> Houston, TX

It just makes sense to start with your mindset. Patrice has truly helped me alter my understandings of money so that I can manage my finances in a much more productive way! She brings so many components together, explains them with a different perspective and inspires you to put them to use in your every day life. Patrice says and I now believe " You Are Your Most Important Resource". So ladies, if you're sick of ending up in the same place, allow her to help you get your financial life in order right now, why wait. With her vast knowledge, her insights and her genuine encouragement, you want regret it! !

> Portia K.
> Executive Assistant
> New Market, AL

Before working with Patrice's Mindset + Money Master Class, I was overwhelmed and didn't know how to even begin organizing my financial life. The Master Class taught me that I had to organize my mind first and foremost to create the solid foundation I'd need for the rest of my life. I have learned to organize my thoughts, prioritize, create focus around my goals and as a result expect my company to grow dramatically! My advice for those thinking of joining her master class: YES! This investment is for your whole life!

> Irani D.
> Choreographer
> Los Angeles, CA

Before the Mindset + Money Master Class, I was lost and trying to figure out just where I was in my financial life. I went through a tough break up that left me mentally and financially exhausted and barely staying afloat. I wanted structure, direction and a little "how to" guidance.

With the Master Class, I have gained the confidence to take my talents and vision to a whole new level. I started a Facebook Fan page for my Southern Cuisine Catering Business, and am well on my way to starting my own Southern Café! After completing my homework assignments in the Mindset + Money Master Class workbook each week, I immediately saw a 45% increase in revenues and look forward to seeing my dreams come true again . . .even at 59 years old!

Joycelyn C.
Caterer
Buckeye, AZ

When I met Patrice in 2011, I was completely depressed and drowning in debt. I spent my entire life doing things the "right way," (college, good job, etc) but I didn't have anything to show for it. I was ashamed and embarrassed and honestly it took a few sessions before I finally told not just Patrice, but myself the truth about how I had gotten into nearly $90k in debt. Patrice helped me figure out why I was emotionally spending and then helped me devise a plan to pay the debt off. Its been two years and I'm half way through my debt and plan on being done in the next 18 months!

Kendara K.
HR Specialist
Atlanta, GA

Before the Mindset + Money Master Class, I had a very sad and negative outlook on money and finances. Although I have acquired more of it in recent years, it always felt like it was flying out of my palms before I could make something of substance happen with it.

Ask yourself:

- *Am I worth doing something different to gain different results?*
- *Am I willing to sit idle and continue to allow my life to be robbed of the fullness it deserves?*
- *Don't I deserve to be debt free and out of struggle?*

When I sat with those questions and I surveyed the type of person Patrice is, her own testimony and her willingness to help others, I had to do this...and the truth is, so do you.

Andrea M.
Independent Consultant
Los Angeles, CA

REAL MONEY ANSWERS®
FOR
EVERY WOMAN

How to Win the Money Game With or Without a Man.

By

THE WISDOM & WEALTH MONEY MAVEN

PATRICE C. WASHINGTON

Seek Wisdom Find Wealth

Atlanta   Los Angeles

Real Money Answers for Every Woman

www.PatriceWashington.com

ISBN # 978-0-9859080-1-0

Published by Seek Wisdom Find Wealth, Mableton, GA 30126

Printed in the United States of America

First Printing, August 2013

Photography by Chad Finley

Cover Design by dw3design.net

Credit to V. Respres, Atlanta, GA

Editing by Candice L. Davis, Atlanta, GA

This book is available at quantity discounts for bulk purchases. For information, please call 404-913-4479.

To my mother, Marie & late grandmother, Kathleen Grace
You are the two women who have made me every
bit of the woman I humbly am today.

To my daughter, Reagan,
Being your mommy is the greatest joy of my life.
I only hope and pray that I lead a life you will always be proud of.

To the hundreds of women who have trusted me to
counsel, coach and mentor them firsthand,
Your stories have inspired me much more than you'll ever know.

To the countless other women I have yet to meet,
May you be blessed by the wisdom within.

PCW

CONTENTS

EVERY WOMAN, at some point in her lifetime, will have to take responsibility for her financial affairs. Whether it comes about voluntarily or involuntarily doesn't change the fact that it *is* inevitable. Studies show that while women earn less in the workplace, they're forced to spend more time and money on the caregiving of children and aging parents, and they live longer than their male counterparts. Studies also show that when women get involved with financial matters such as investing, they tend to be better at it than men, due to innate qualities like patience and self-control.

So why then are countless women forced into managing their finances, rather than naturally gravitating to it? Lack of both formal and informal education surrounding the topic could be one reason. Another argument I've heard is that "old school" gender roles suggest that men handle finances while women just trust that all is well. I'd venture to say that this mode of thinking isn't really "old school" but is still prevalent and perpetuated in a modern society which praises any show with the term "housewives" in the title, even when those women are successful and professionally established in their own right.

My own journey with personal finance began in 2003, shortly after my college graduation. What I thought would be just another night of Bible study turned into a financial seminar that would change the course of my life. I sat down with my bills and realized that at barely twenty-two years old I had racked up $18,000 of credit card debt. I saw the numbers, but it still took a few hours to register that I was in way over my head. I'd received tons of grants, scholarships, school loans, and parental assistance. I even worked a full-time job through my entire collegiate career. I never had to put a textbook on credit. Unlike many of my friends, I never needed a cash advance to cover the rent. There were no designer purses to show for the debt, not even a lavish spring break trip to reminisce upon. Making one small poor decision after another, over the course of less than four years, led me to that moment. And I wanted out!

Once I began to do the hard work of getting my finances in order, I realized my journey didn't begin at eighteen years old with the free t-shirt I got for signing up for a credit card. It began many years before. It began when I sat in Sunday school and heard people talk about money being the root of all evil. It began at four years old when I carried my mom's expired credit cards in my Betty Boop purse, because it made me feel grown up. It began when my dad, who knew a lot about money, gave me an allowance but never had a conversation about just how to spend it. All innocent experiences, but detrimental, nonetheless.

The money journey for each of us begins well before the lay-off, the divorce, the bankruptcy, or the foreclosure. It begins with subtle, indirect conversations during childhood. The human brain isn't fully developed until the age of twenty-one. In childhood and adolescence, we can't fully understand the long-term consequences of our actions. All a child knows is what they learn by observing the world around them. For example, I learned early on how to avoid what I thought to be the annoying calls of a creditor. As a six-year-old, I was the family's caller ID, answering those calls only to lie and assert "so and so isn't here right now" while someone nodded to me, "Good girl." in the background. The lesson here: the way to deal with collection calls is not to deal with them.

Please know I'm not sharing this so you can go out and blame your pastors and parents. Now that you're an adult, this is all about you. And besides, the best thing about childhood is that it's over! The best is yet to come, and despite how the story began, you have an opportunity to write the happy ending you desire.

What you'll read over the next several pages are simple-to-grasp concepts and easy-to-implement solutions. You don't have to be a money maven to live a life with adequate savings, peace of mind, and freedom from harassing creditors. But you will have to take action! This journey is a process that takes hard work and effort on your part. Being sound financially is a personal choice, hence the term *personal finance*. By implementing the lessons you learn here, as well as continuing to seek out answers to your most pressing money questions, you establish your commitment to defining and determining your own destiny.

Will this guide answer all the financial questions you'll ever have? Absolutely not. At least I hope you don't stop here. My goal is to introduce you to basic financial knowledge that other women in your life may not have shared. This is truly just a start, or maybe a refresher course for some of you. My hope is that you'll be so inspired that you'll naturally desire to learn more and more.

Whether you're a busy wife, single mother, college student, young professional, or mature woman of a certain age, this book was written to help you achieve your personal finance goals at any level. You'll find answers to most of the questions that many women are afraid to admit they can't answer. But after counseling and coaching literally hundreds of men and women, I knew exactly what to include. So cheers to your success. It's time to play a bigger game and master this journey—with or without a man! ☺

HOW TO USE THIS BOOK

After counseling and coaching hundreds of women, I began to take note of the recurring themes that came up in individual and group sessions. Despite age, geographic location, religious beliefs, educational background, marital status, or income level, most women share identical concerns and questions about their money.

How can I earn more?
How can I give more?
How can I manage it better?
What can I do to become a better example for my children?
Do I have to give up my entire lifestyle to be a good money manager?

If you can identify with any of those questions, you've picked up the right resource. *Real Money Answers for Every Woman* was written like any of the titles you'll find in my *Real Money Answers* series. Although it's written in a question and answer format, it can be read like any other book, straight through from beginning to end. Reading it in order will give you a solid understanding of the personal finance issues most common among women on the path to establishing or reestablishing a positive relationship with their money.

On the other hand, this book was also written to be a resource guide for you to get straight to the areas you might need the most help with at any particular point in life. It's written in four subject specific sections to help you quickly get your questions answered. The sections build on each other in natural progression and follow the format of my women's coaching program, the *Mindset + Money Master Class®*. The four guiding principles are Create Wealthy Habits, Earn More Money, Manage Money Wisely, and Relationships and Money. They represent my entire philosophy about personal finance success, which laid the foundation for how I was able to get out of $18,000 of credit card debt in less than twenty-four months. Beyond that, they're the principles that have helped women across the world actually achieve personal finance goals they once only dreamed could be reached.

Because it's such an easy read, if you have any questions about a particular topic, you may as well read the entire section. That way you can begin to commit the information to memory and put it into practice. As you'll soon learn, results are based on actions, actions on thoughts, and thoughts on beliefs, and beliefs are formed by the information you allow into your mind. In order for you to achieve the intended result of financial independence, you'll have to actually apply the answers you read on these pages.

To jumpstart your journey, I suggest you get a special notebook or three-ring binder to keep your notes in order. Personally, I dedicate a journal each year to my professional, personal, and financial development. As you encounter personal reflection assignments or other concepts that strike a chord for you, record your thoughts there. This will show you how much you've learned and accomplished in any given period of time. You can't do it all in one day, but as I say to every woman who works with me personally, progress beats perfection any day. Enjoy.

LOOK FOR THESE HELPFUL NOTES THROUGHOUT

Quotes and
expressions to
remember

Savings tips
or financial
illustrations

Statistics or
stories that need
to stick

Positive
declarations
to repeat and
remember

CREATE WEALTHY HABITS

Personal finance success is less about what you actually know and more about how much of what you know you implement in your daily life.

THE REAL MONEY ANSWERS series was created to give you quick, simple, practical, and real answers to some of your most pressing money questions. By virtue of the fact that you picked up a book like this, I already expect you to flip to the obvious questions about credit cards, home buying, student loans, entrepreneurship, and the like. But I've been around long enough to know that I also have to provide answers to the questions you may not even think to ask at this stage in your journey. *Create Wealthy Habits* will give you what I consider to be the absolute foundation of personal finance success. It's about teaching you the basic principle that any successful person will share with you: True success starts on the inside; the outside is merely the byproduct.

We are creatures of habit. Period. Most people understand this on the surface. The part they don't get, however, is that habits come in two forms: doing and not doing. Many of us can think of the things we actively do each day as habits, which may be either good or bad. But when you *don't* do the things you know you should be doing, you're also practicing the often unnoticed habit of simply not doing, which can be just as detrimental. As I often tell my clients, "Stop telling me what you are *trying* to do.

Real TALK

You're either doing or you're not doing. There is no in-between.

You're either doing or you're not doing. There is *no* in-between."

If you aren't practicing wealthy habits, then you're more than likely practicing un-wealthy habits. Once you acknowledge that there's no in between and begin to take action, you can move onward and upward. The choice is ultimately yours.

So get ready to learn the stuff you didn't even know you needed to know. Get ready to create, and more importantly, implement wealthy habits!

MONEY MINDSETS, ATTITUDES & MYTHS

Building wealth has 100% nothing to do with money; it has 100% everything to do with you and your mindset towards money.

THE STATEMENT ABOVE IS how I've opened every financial talk I've given for the last several years. Initially, I see people smirk as if that statement itself is the greatest myth they've ever heard. You may be no different. Who can blame you? For countless years you've heard, witnessed, and experienced mindsets, attitudes, and myths about money that just don't add up.

Listen up and pay very close attention here. Contrary to popular belief, financial success isn't really about money at all. It's about recognizing where these beliefs were formed and reconditioning them to support the life you desire, deserve, and have declared you will work diligently to bring forth.

You should know we all have those lies, large and small, that we tell ourselves to justify why we do the things we do. The reality is, however, that every single decision you make is either helping you or hurting you. There really isn't much grey area there. Whether or not you choose to acknowledge it now really doesn't matter. Your long-term financial standing will inevitably show you what you deemed important during your short-term decision-making.

The next few pages are geared toward proving that there is absolutely no coincidence that you have this book in your hands. Uncover the lies—I mean, mindsets, attitudes, and myths—that have been holding you back from financial freedom.

I DESERVE IT.

Do you work hard? Of course you do. Do you deserve to indulge every once in a while? Eh, maybe. The real question is whether another pair of new black shoes is really worth staying in debt? Sometimes you may need to ask yourself, "As much as I deserve _____, don't I deserve to be debt free even more?" If your answer is, "No, I *deserve* to work my entire adult life and still end up with nothing at the age of retirement," then by all means, close this book ASAP and continue on with your old mindset. Buy all the shoes you want and throw in a pair for me! Remember, it's not the one "I deserve it" conversation that will shatter your financial future. It's the constant conversations you have with yourself to justify that kind of spending that hurt you in the long run.

Real TALK
Every decision you make is either helping you or hurting you.

IT WAS AN EMERGENCY.

Let's get clear about what emergencies are. Merriam-Webster defines the term emergency as *"A serious, unexpected, and often dangerous situation requiring immediate action."* With that being said, dipping into your emergency fund (or opportunity fund, which you'll learn more about later) for expenses that you were fully aware were coming up is NOT an emergency. Cars wear and tear. You were aware of that when you drove off the lot. Car registration is just a fact of life. And if you live in a state like Georgia, which makes sure you know when your registration is due by billing you on your birthday each year, there's no excuse. It's important to make every expense a line item on your budget. Even those things that are quarterly or annual expenditures can be planned for on a monthly basis.

I BOUGHT IT ON SALE.

Oh, yeah! We've all fallen for this rationale at one time or another. The reality is most people are in debt because of STUFF. It's impossible to get out of debt if you're committed to buying more and more stuff instead of truly being financially free.

One way to avoid this trap is to stop walking around the mall and window shopping and stop surfing your favorite online sites. I'd even go as far as unsubscribing from all of the tempting newsletters with the "great deals" in your e-mail inbox each morning. Instead of convincing yourself that you're saving, begin to ask yourself, "Do I really need this?" Remember that buying something you don't need is never better than saving money for your actual needs. Think of it this way, when you're on a weight loss diet, is it really wise to walk through food courts scouting out samples of fresh baked cinnamon rolls and greasy pizza? Exactly.

A COUPLE BUCKS NEVER HURT ANYONE.

Speak for yourself. I heard someone say once that the $1 menu is the quickest way to go broke. It's the small charges that add up and inevitably break the budget and the bank. I have more clients that get caught up in $34 overdraft fees for a quick $5 swipe at the gas station than anything else. Ever enjoy a $36 bottle of water or candy bar? Yeah, nothing is that darn good. If millionaires are concerned about watching the bottom line and keeping up with every penny, I suggest you start sweating the small stuff, ma'am. Again, it's important that you get in the habit of asking yourself, "Do I *really* need this?" or "Can I find this somewhere else for less?" even with the purchases that may seem like no big deal.

Real TALK

Millionaires keep up with every penny, and you should, too.

IF I MADE MORE MONEY, THIS WOULD BE EASIER.

Just stop. No it wouldn't. Without discipline, you could double your income and still have tons of debt and no savings. Hell, you could triple it this year and be worse off than you are today in less than three years. How do I know this? We've all heard of the entertainers, athletes, and my favorite, lottery winners, who end up flat broke and in deep debt despite having access to millions. Don't assume that more money is the answer. If you refuse to dig deep and get serious about managing $100, then having $100,000, whether you won it or earned it, will not all of a sudden make you better with money. I know it's hard to believe, but just trust me on this one.

I'LL START LATER.

Now this is one of the ultimate myths that we fall for. I love it when women attempt to explain to me that they're going to get on their money game after such and such. After the New Year, the new job, the new husband, the new or next anything. In case you can't relate yet, let me tell you what the typical excuses—I mean "rational reasons"—sound like and what the people who hear them are probably thinking.

> *Oh, it's at the top of my New Year's resolution list!*
> Awesome, but it's June. Six months? Really?

> *I'll start paying off debt after the holidays.*
> Of course. You need time to pile on some more debt first, right?

> *My future husband is going to take care of the money.*
> And if Prince Charming never comes, then what, lady?

> *Once I get my income tax refund next year, I'm going to just pay everything.*
> Yeah, so no discipline implemented there. With no strategy and no savings plan, you'll be back in debt by June.

Get the point? I hope so, because here's the problem with continuing to delay things. For starters, something more important or necessary will always be going on or coming up in your life. Second, you can't keep banking on what anyone else may come in and do or not do tomorrow.

So what are you *really* waiting for? It's easy to *talk* about change, but when will you take action and just start already? If you don't start today, years may go by, and the next so-and-so will never come.

I DON'T MAKE ENOUGH TO SAVE.

Ouch! I've been bitten by this one before. One of the lines I once told myself and probably hear most often is, "I can't afford to save, pay down debt, blah, blah, blah." The line I can now offer back is, "You can't afford NOT to save!"

When it comes to saving, you have to start somewhere, and you have to start today.

I recently sat down with an advisor friend from one of the country's largest financial firms. He told me that his most successful clients all have one thing in common: they are disciplined about their savings and clear about their values and goals. He shared candidly that some of the families with the best portfolios are those that have earned less than $80,000 per year, but have been saving and investing for decades.

The very folks who believe they can't save somehow manage to give the bank $34 per overdraft fee each month or $29 for late credit card payments. I'd venture to say, if you can pay the bank money every month involuntarily, there should be a way to squeeze out a few bucks to give your savings account voluntarily. It doesn't matter whether you start putting just an extra $10 towards paying off your debt. You have to start somewhere, and you have to start *today*.

I DON'T KNOW ANYTHING ABOUT MONEY.

I'm sorry. Is that still supposed to fly these days? With search engines like Google at your fingertips, I'm not sure you'll get any sympathy on this one. You don't have to be an "expert" to know that if you spend less than you earn, save money, invest money, and plan for the future, then you'll likely be better off in the future. This timeless wisdom has been passed on for generations by ancestors who didn't have access to the education you've enjoyed.

Isn't it worth the time spent doing a little extra research to get rid of harassing phone calls, have money saved, and have greater options in case of an emergency? There are far too many personal finance books, blogs, professional coaches, and non-profit counseling agencies offering complimentary classes on credit and money management for you to remain in the dark. Find a few resources that work for you, and just stick with it. You have to start somewhere.

IT'S GOOD DEBT.

Where did this ridiculous rumor originate? Despite what you've heard, student loans and mortgages are *not* good debt. There's no such thing, in my humble opinion. The best debt is the debt you don't owe anymore! If you're only keeping your mortgage for the tax write-off, try this: give more to your place of worship or favorite charity. You can write that off, without all the wasted interest payments.

The only good debt, is debt you don't owe anymore.

Are there times in life when you'll need to leverage debt to advance? Of course. But when you classify something as "good," there's no intention or intensity behind your desire to get rid of it. When you understand that repaying someone considerably more than you borrowed is a waste of your hard earned money, you can get serious about a plan to pay off the debt.

I'M JUST A GIVING PERSON.

By nature, women are givers. And I really believe that's a great thing. It's one of the characteristics I love most about us. But there came a point when I had to ask myself a few questions about this giving nature.

- *Am I really helping the people I'm giving to over and over again, or am I hurting them?*
- *How much more could I give if I didn't have all this debt?*
- *Can I keep giving to the point of my own deprivation?*

The sooner you tell yourself the truth, the sooner you can change your financial life.

I'm not sure about you, but those were tough questions for me to answer. And even tougher was the thought of having to tell the recipients of the giving that enough was enough. Until I understood that I could give in other ways—my time, my talents, my wisdom—I was in bondage to this type of thinking.

I hope a few of these mindsets, attitudes, and myths have struck a chord, as they were designed to do. Now that you know the thoughts and beliefs that have been misguiding you and causing the personal finance results you've had so far, it's time to learn how to change them. The sooner we can tell ourselves the truth, the sooner we'll be able to take charge and change our financial lives once and for all!

REFLECT | What money lies have you been telling yourself?

WEALTH BEGINS WITHIN

THE BACK OF MY business cards once read: *Changing roots, changing fruits, changing lives.* When I handed them out, people always asked me to explain what it meant. In a nutshell, fruits represent the results we see in our lives each day. Your bank account balance, where you live, the opportunities that come your way, and the relationships you currently have are all your fruits or outcomes.

When people desire to make a change in these areas, they falsely assume that if they switch banks, or move to a new city, or dump the person they're dating, that everything in their lives will improve. But what happens when the same results creep back in, even in a new environment or with a new person? Well, you end up with the same fruits. Until you change your roots, the stuff deep down on the inside that causes you to think or act a certain way, you will never change your fruits, and you will never change your life.

Think of it this way. If you reap what you sow, can you really keep planting apple seeds and expecting oranges? Can you really keep tally of your expenses in your head and expect to not overdraft? Can you really continue to not save money and expect your emergencies to not become drama-filled catastrophes? Can you really continue to buy your children everything under the sun and expect them to respect money? . . . I'll wait.

This isn't about just learning how to write out a budget or balance a checkbook. It's not about starting a business or earning a promotion. The desire and discipline to do all of those things consistently and successfully must come from somewhere else. It starts with your thoughts, values, beliefs, and mindset. Your road to wealth begins within.

WHAT THE HECK IS A FINANCIAL BLUEPRINT, ANYWAY?

I used to say that our financial blueprints were handed down to us by our parents, almost like a strand of DNA. Then people started claiming their bad habits were actually hereditary. The truth is no one is born with a particular attitude toward money. You were taught, just like we all were, how to think about and handle money matters. These subconscious beliefs, ideals, thoughts, and actions are what create your financial blueprint.

In addition to your parents, these money influences could include siblings, friends, teachers, and religious doctrine or leaders you were exposed to during adolescence. Nevertheless, unless they're first recognized and then reconditioned, it's very likely that the lessons and habits you learned as a child may still be causing you to subconsciously sabotage your own success with money.

When determining your financial blueprint, consider the following factors.

VERBAL INFLUENCES: What did you hear about money, wealth, and rich people when you were growing up? Did anyone ever say things like *filthy rich, money can't buy love, the poor will be close to God, money is the root of all evil, it takes money to make money,* or *you only need enough to get by?*

_____

_____

_____

_____

MODELING: What did you witness in regards to how your parents obtained, managed, and allocated money? Did they have any systems or budgets in place? Was money a source of joy or stress for your family? Did your parents argue about money often or sit down and plan together?

_____

_____

_____

_____

SPECIFIC INCIDENTS: What experiences do you remember about money, wealth, and rich people? Were you embarrassed at a cash register when a credit card was declined? Did you experience eviction notices or utility services being interrupted? Ever teased for not having the latest clothing or electronics?

_____

_____

_____

_____

After taking a moment to record your initial thoughts, give yourself additional time to reflect. Truly consider each one of these categories and complete the following exercise for each influence.

AWARENESS: Reflect upon the things that were said, the ways of being you witnessed and a specific incident you experienced in regards to money and wealth. Please note that not everyone endures negative experiences. Some people undergo feelings of financial guilt for not having grown up in difficult financial circumstances. Write down how your life today may be identical to, or exactly opposite to, each of the things you remember.

_____

_____

_____

_____

UNDERSTANDING: Write down the effect these words, habits, and incidents from your youth have had on your financial life.

_____

_____

_____

_____

DISASSOCIATION: Separate who you are today from what you witnessed as a child. That life was what your parents chose, and you have a choice in the present moment to be different. How will you choose to break this cycle in your family? What steps can you take to be a better example and influence for the young people around you?

_____

_____

_____

_____

MY PARENTS DIDN'T TEACH ME ANYTHING ABOUT MONEY. NOW WHAT?

ANSWER #1: Welcome to the club.

ANSWER #2: Accept it and move on.

I know these probably seem like cruel answers, but the bottom line is everyone has something they can legitimately blame their parents for doing, or not doing, that negatively impacted their life. At some point, however, you have to be an adult and let it go, if you're truly to move on with your own life. Becoming wealthy, getting out of debt, saving, investing, and the like cannot take place until you take ownership of your life. Let's face it. The blame game is just not sexy. It's also not a trait of a wealthy woman on the road to accomplishing her dreams.

Remember, your parents are someone's children, too. They may have learned their poor financial habits from your beloved Gram and Pops. (See: *What the heck is a financial blueprint, anyway?*) Just be happy you have a chance to break that generational cycle. All you can do now is make sure you do your part to expose your family to a totally different mindset and blueprint towards money and wealth-building principles.

It doesn't matter how old you are. If you're still alive, then you've still got time to correct the wrongs of your childhood!

REFLECT | Who have you been blaming for your money mistakes?

HOW DO I START CHANGING THE WAY I THINK ABOUT MONEY?

This is no easy task. Remember, you may have grown up hearing, seeing, and forming a lot of negative money and wealth-creation habits. (See: *What the heck is a financial blueprint, anyway?*) But a part of being wealthy is having the mindset that money is an important tool that, when utilized properly, can assist you in truly creating the life you want. When used improperly it can become a source of anxiety, stress, and strife.

☑AFFIRM

Money is an important tool that can help me create the life I want.

The difference between poor people and wealthy people is simply the way they think about money. The only way to progress and move past your past is to replace your previous thinking with a new and fresh perspective. I believe wholeheartedly in using positive affirmations as one tool to do so. Below are a few samples of what I used to change my thinking.

When I first began my journey, I created simple statements I could recite in the shower or while I was driving to the office each day.

Old Way of Thinking:	*I'm clueless about money. I don't even know where to start.*
New Way of Thinking:	I am ready, willing, and able to manage my money!
Old Way of Thinking:	*It's just a penny. That's nothing.*
New Way of Thinking:	The cents matter just as much as the dollars do! I love ALL money!
Old Way of Thinking:	*Money is so hard to come by.*
New Way of Thinking:	Money flows to me easily, freely, and often!

If you're on my mailing list, you know that each week I send out original Wisdom & Wealth Affirmations and personal reflection exercises to help you grow your mind and your money. While I love my one-liners, I also share longer affirming statements, so that readers can get clear about the full context of what they're declaring over their lives. Below is a sample of some of my favorites.

I AM the CEO of my life.

I set the strategy, goals, and vision for my life. **I own my successes. I own my failures. I understand that success is going from failure to failure without loss of enthusiasm.** When I experience a major challenge, I re-invent myself in the marketplace. I protect my brand at all cost. Quality control is in my hands. **I choose team players that work to fulfill the mission and vision.** I fire those who do not get the job done. I focus only on the activities which produce positive returns. I take 100% responsibility for the outcomes in my life.

I AM the CEO of my life.

Powerful stuff, right?

Now let's go a step beyond just thinking these types of thoughts. What do you think could happen if instead of constantly whining, complaining, and focusing on the things you don't want, you began speaking these positive things over your life? Remember, what you verbalize you magnify and magnetize in your own life.

REFLECT | What could you manifest if you changed your way of thinking today? What is the one affirmation you know you need to incorporate into your daily life immediately?

Visit www.PatriceWashington.com to register for weekly Wisdom & Wealth Affirmations to help you grow your mind and money.

WHAT CAN I DO TO CREATE WEALTHIER HABITS?

I have to reiterate here that most people understand the idea that we humans are "creatures of habit." The part they don't get, however, is that when you don't do anything to change negative habits, then you are already in the habit of not doing. I spend a lot of time, actually more time than I care to admit, asking people to stop telling me what they're *trying* to do. You're either doing or you're not doing. There's really no wiggle room here, ladies. Either you have doing habits or not-doing habits. For example, reading is one thing, but being in the habit of doing something with what you read is a completely different story. Knowledge doesn't create success. Action creates success. So make sure you implement the principles you read below. Full answers on how to do so are found throughout the book.

Real TALK
There's no trying to create wealthy habits. You're either doing it or not doing it.

GET CLEAR ABOUT YOUR GOALS

It's impossible to get what you want if you aren't exactly sure of what you want. I love the verse Habakkuk 2:2, which tells us to "write down your vision and make it plain." You need to be clear about your intentions in order to bring them forth. You must write them down and be as concrete as possible with any details, especially those dealing with numbers or financial objectives. You'll be amazed at how opportunities come about and begin to lead you in the direction of your goal. (For complete steps on financial goal-setting, see: *How do I set financial goals I can achieve?*)

DECLARE A PURPOSE

You have to know the *why* behind what you want. Without declaring a purpose, you'll continue to live in the moment and blindly throw money away, or even worse, lie to yourself about why you're not closer to where you'd like to be. (See: *Money Mindsets, Attitudes & Myths*.) Knowing the *why* of what you're doing, will keep you focused on reaching both long-term and short-term goals. Your purpose helps you prioritize your actions and invest in activities that push you closer to what you say you want. (For complete steps to understanding your *why*, see: *How do I know what I really value?*)

COMMIT TO A LIFESTYLE OF LEARNING

Education doesn't stop after the diploma or the degree. Did you know the difference between where you are today and where you will be in five years is directly related to the people you associate with and the books you read?

In his book, *How Rich People Think*, Steve Siebold shares a very sad, yet true observation. "Walk into a wealthy person's home and one of

Real TALK
Knowledge doesn't create success. Action creates success.

the first things you'll see is an extensive library of books they've used to educate themselves on how to become more successful." He continues, "The middle class reads novels, tabloids and entertainment magazines."

Wealthy people commit to a lifestyle of education, and non-wealthy people commit to a lifestyle of simply being entertained. Even if you don't categorize yourself as a reader, it's time to find the mode of learning that works for you. You can attend seminars and conferences, dial into teleconferences, log on to webinars, or invest in coaching or finding a mentor or mastermind group. Figure out what works for you, but commit from this day forward that you will never stop learning.

UNDERSTAND YOUR VALUE

Understanding your value allows you to create wealth in two ways. The first way is that you learn how to respond to people or situations that threaten your financial success. When you don't understand your value, your own self-worth, you're at risk of associating money with different thoughts and actions that don't support your long-term vision. You allow yourself to be taken advantage of by mooching family members, because you falsely believe you're giving and/or receiving love or some other desired emotion.

The other side of understanding your value relates to knowing what to charge for your service or product. You're blessed with unique abilities, gifts, skills, and talents, just as every person is. Selling yourself short is an insult to God. He gives us the ability to produce wealth, but when we don't maximize that potential to the fullest, we can't turn around and beg God for more financially. Once you understand and declare your value, you'll be much more confident in having the difficult, but necessary, conversations with loved ones or charging what you're worth and communicating that to potential clientele.

GET VISUAL

Most inventions first began as an image in the inventor's mind. In 1903, when the first airplane was created, Orville and Wilbur Wright had only a mental image of what this flying machine would become. Until they put this image on paper and created a sketch and a blueprint, it was still just a dream. Reaching your personal finance goals cannot continue to simply be a dream. You need a blueprint. You need a visual representation of your financial goals.

I have always used picture journals and dream boards as focal points in turning imagination into reality. Find magazine photos or pictures online and post them where you can see them daily. Use the power of your visual sense to keep you focused on your goal. This focus is what will keep you motivated over the long haul.

MAINTAIN A GRATEFUL SPIRIT

I often say, "What you verbalize you magnify and magnetize in your life." When you're in a space that promotes whining, complaining, and dwelling on the negative aspects of your life, you repel financial success, and any other type of success. When you remain grateful for those things, no matter how few, which are going right in your life, you allow yourself to find wealth in whatever situation you may be experiencing at any given moment.

AFFIRM

I possess all of my needs, as well as my wants.

When you are grateful for what you already have, as well as those things you desire, you become happier and healthier and can attract more of the same.

DEVELOP A "SO WHAT, NOW WHAT?" ATTITUDE

The reality is that obstacles are going to be thrown your way, no matter how much positive thinking and prayer you use. Instead of allowing life's distractions to throw you off course, you have to accept them, learn the lesson, and move on, continuously pressing toward your goals. When you can look life head-on and say, "This challenge has occurred, but what can I do now to move on?" you will reach goals you never thought were possible. Taking on this type of attitude teaches you to act in spite of your own doubts and fears or ridicule from others. When you press on despite the unexpected, you build courage and can take down challenges one by one!

Real MONEY

When you press on in the face of obstacles, you strengthen your ability to take on future challenges.

GIVE WELL, RECEIVE WELL

Believe it or not, many of us are neither good at giving nor at receiving. You may think you are, but if you really study your habits in everyday things, you may be shocked at what you discover.

You may feel like a great giver when you help a relative, but when was the last time you gave to an absolute stranger? You might be quick to walk another offering to the altar at your church where people know you, but when's the last time you picked a charity to support because you really believed in the good work being done by the organization? Truly good givers give to uplift and champion others, even when no one is looking.

Think about the last time someone complimented your shoes. Without blinking, you might've instantly gone into "these old things" or the "they were only $20" conversation. Perhaps you felt uncomfortable and tried to take all the thunder out of the compliment. Women that receive well will simply thank the person and let the warm gesture give them a nice boost of energy.

The bottom line is giving and receiving work in perfect harmony. You must give in order to receive, and the more you receive, the more you are expected to give again. Have you noticed how philanthropic the world's wealthiest people are? As much as you've heard about their giving, you don't see Oprah or Bill Gates running out of money.

REFLECT | What wealthy habits do you need to begin working on immediately?

WHERE DO I FIND THE MOTIVATION TO CHANGE MY HABITS?

I was blown away the first time someone asked me this question. I had never really thought about it, and honestly, I still can't say that I have a definitive answer. This is one of those questions that could be answered "to each her own."

I've found that, like me, my clients are usually motivated by the past, the future, or a hybrid of the two. I didn't grow up in the best neighborhood. I lived with my mother and grandmother above a storefront on a main street in South Central Los Angeles. I've heard and seen drive-by shootings firsthand, and I've witnessed people shooting up drugs in the alley behind my building. When I was very young, these things, along with other experiences I won't even begin to share, motivated me to work hard, go to college, and declare that I was *not* coming back.

Now that I'm a mother myself, a huge part of my motivation is making sure my children never have to experience the negative elements or difficult environments I did. I'm also motivated by the fact that I enjoy a certain lifestyle and would prefer to hang on to it until I exit life stage left. I've been there, done that with the harassing phone calls from creditors, the money wasted on overdraft fees, and the arguments with people about finances. Frankly, I've reached a point of being sick and tired of being sick and tired, and I really could do without going back to that place.

REFLECT | What will you use as your personal motivation to really achieve your financial goals this time around?

I HAVE SO MUCH FEAR AROUND FINANCIAL MATTERS. HOW DO I GET OVER THAT?

Believe it or not, you're not alone. Fear is the number one emotion that comes up for most people, men and women alike, when money becomes the topic of conversation. You may have so much anxiety around your finances you don't even open bills anymore. Maybe you crumple your ATM receipt quickly to avoid facing the balance printed on the bottom. Or maybe you avoid direct conversations with friends and family after being taken advantage of so many times in the past.

Whatever the cause of your fear, you have to work through it and manage it, or abandon it altogether, to make progress. Financial therapy for individuals, couples, and families who desire to understand the emotional triggers and experiences that may cause them to fear finances and therefore make poor financial decisions is a relatively new and growing field. It may help you communicate better about money and uncover irrational financial

AFFIRM

I view every limitation as a new possibility.

fears while empowering you to move forward with your financial plans. If you think your need goes further than simply reading a few online resources, don't be afraid to check out a financial therapist in your area. Visit www.financialtherapyassociation.org.

REFLECT | How much time and energy do you spend worrying about money daily? How could you spend that time more productively?

SETTING THE FOUNDATION

THE LAST TIME YOU decided to get your finances in order, where did you start? Perhaps with a copy of your credit report or a freshly printed budget from your Microsoft Excel templates? Typically, when people start working on their finances, they kick things off with these sorts of external activities and completely ignore any internal factors. They soon find all this action is only busywork. Their motivation fizzles out, because there's no foundation sustaining it.

The truth is that building a successful foundation with finances begins on the inside, not the outside. It's not so much about your budgeting skills as it is about your beliefs concerning money. Personal finance guru, Barbara Stanny put it best when she broke down the three core levels on which financial success is based.

The first level is the Inner Work of Wealth, which deals with your mindset. This means understanding your fears, beliefs, and attitudes surrounding money, wealth, and financial success, as well as understanding where they originated. This gets to the root of how you feel about money. Some people assume that we all *love* money, but many of us have a totally different relationship with it. Every change in life must begin with a decision, and until you can recognize the *what* and *where* of your relationship with money, you'll never really make the decision to implement the steps necessary to recondition yourself.

The second level is the Outer Work of Wealth, which deals with developing money-managing skills. This covers earning money, including understanding your worth and charging appropriately for it, whether

Real TALK

Until you understand your money mindset, you'll never be able to change your relationship with money.

you choose to work in your own business or in someone else's. It also includes the way you save, spend, and invest. Understanding your natural inclination in these activities is a part of discovering your personal money style, which is key in setting the foundation for your success.

The third and final level is the Higher Work of Wealth. This is where we obtain our sense of giving and helping others. It also dictates our relationships and conversations that involve money.

If you were to see it as a hierarchy, the higher Work is at the top, and it's easiest to do when it has a strong foundation, in terms of mindset and skill set, to sustain it.

WHAT IS PERSONAL FINANCE, REALLY?

If you're embarrassed by that question, you shouldn't be. More people should actually ask it, and more personal finance gurus should stop assuming that everybody knows the answer. Personal finance deals with your individual relationship with money. It serves as your financial outline, speaking

AFFIRM

I am ready, willing, and able to manage my money wisely and successfully!

to the ways you obtain, budget, save, spend, and manage monetary resources. These behaviors are assessed at various stages throughout your lifetime, taking into account a mixture of external financial variables, like home value depreciations or stock market declines, and major life events, like getting your first job or getting married.

Some of the major components of personal finance may include checking and savings accounts, credit cards, consumer and student loans, investment principles, income tax management, and much more, depending on which phase of life you're in. Despite which stage you fall into at any given time in your life, a positive relationship with money forces you to continuously assess your responses to important questions.

These questions are the foundation for creating a personal financial plan:

How much money and how many financial assets do I possess today?
How much money will I need at various points in the future?
How do I go about getting that money in the present?

The most basic plan will always include these five steps:

1. Assessment: *Where are you now?*

2. Goal Setting: *Where do you want to be?*

3. Creating a Plan: *How will you get there?*

4. Execution: *Take action and make it happen.*

5. Re-Assessment: *Repeat the process regularly.*

Use the worksheet in Appendix C to complete your personal financial plan.

WHAT IF I'M NOT REALLY A FINANCE TYPE OF PERSON?

No matter what our profession or path in life, our personal finances are the one thing that we all have to manage and control. This is not about what you like to do. This is what you must do to take control of your life and your destiny. If you've fooled yourself into thinking that because you're "creative," or "artsy," or a "social entrepreneur" you don't have to worry about money, then just quit now. No, seriously. Stop reading, because you clearly missed the part about reflecting upon and identifying the lies you might be telling yourself.

AFFIRM

I have an appetite for continuous learning.

If you're not really a finance type of person, then make yourself one, and quickly! That type of mentality is not how a wealthy, successful person thinks. If you're thinking you'll be fine, God will provide, you'll just hit the lottery one day, blah, blah, blah, then this book—*all the books in the world*—won't help you. You might be uncomfortable hearing that, but somebody had to tell you. It is what it is. And if you're not ready, all I ask is that you not toss me up on the shelf. At least pass me on to someone you know that's ready to be a finance type of person.

WHAT IS THE MOST IMPORTANT FINANCIAL PRINCIPLE I SHOULD KNOW?

I probably sound like a broken record, but the most important financial principle to remember is that to achieve success in your finances, your mindset toward wealth creation must be on the correct setting. Your thoughts, actions, and feelings around money must be shaped on the inside before positive results manifest on the outside.

As I often say, your roots create your fruits. No matter how much money you accumulate in your life, if you're not ready to receive it on the inside, your outside will never allow you to keep it. Being financially sound takes having a mindset that you're determined to seek out those opportunities to learn more about what you know you don't know, as well as those things you have no idea you don't know.

Some time ago, I heard a wonderful New Year's sermon in which the pastor asserted it's extremely important to realize how important *who you need to be* is in relationship to setting goals for where you want to go and what you want to have. The pastor shared that many people have gifts and talents that will take them to celebrated places in life—places where their characters can never maintain nor sustain them.

Is that deep or what? Think about the entertainers, athletes, and other celebrated figures in society who've amassed great fortunes only to end up on the E network's *True Hollywood Story* explaining how they lost it all. Don't shake your head or point your finger. You're no different! If you don't begin digging deep and strengthening your roots now, tomorrow's fruits will never change, and while the life you desire may be attainable, it will never be sustainable.

If you plan to be successful on this very often sacrificial journey, then you must make up your mind right now that where you want to go and who you want to be outweigh what anyone else thinks about you. Decide now that you will maintain a "whatever it takes" attitude. Resolve that you will not place a lot of weight on what anyone else thinks of your plan.

UN REAL

More than 70% of Americans are living paycheck to paycheck.

Understand that on this journey you must refuse to be "normal," living paycheck to paycheck like most Americans. Decide today that you will take control of your mindset in order to take control of your life. *Are you ready?*

HOW DO YOU DEFINE WEALTH?

The dictionary defines wealth this way:

> **wealth** (wĕ lth) *n.*
> 1. **a.** An abundance of valuable material possessions or resources; riches.
>   **b.** The state of being rich; affluence.
> 2. All goods and resources having value in terms of exchange or use.
> 3. A great amount; a profusion: *a wealth of advice.*

I've also heard many different explanations of wealth from a biblical standpoint. Many are positive, but many others offer a negative view, portraying rich people as miserable and painting a picture of the unspeakable joy the poor.

AFFIRM

I deserve to be wealthy because of the value I add to others.

When deciding what you choose to believe, consider the following questions.

If God gave us the ability to produce wealth, why would it be evil?

If God calls upon us to help the poor, how can we do it when we put ourselves in a position that doesn't even allow us to help ourselves?

If God calls us to leave an inheritance to our children's children, how can we possibly do that when we have more debt than we do assets?

It just doesn't add up to me, so I choose to believe that God wants me to be wealthy because of the value that I add to His people, and I will be a good steward of all that I'm blessed to receive.

You can create your own definition. After all, it sets the foundation for how *you* move forward, so get clear about it, and quickly!

REFLECT | What does financial wealth look like to you?

HOW DO I SET FINANCIAL GOALS I CAN ACHIEVE?

There is a distinct difference between hoping, wishing, dreaming, and even praying for the things you want and actually setting goals that will allow you to achieve your financial dreams.

When most people set financial goals, they sound something like this:

- *I want to improve my credit score.*
- *I'd like to save more.*
- *It would be nice to pay off debt.*

Undefined goals are nothing more than dream killers.

Those dry, bland, and grossly vague goals don't work when you're looking for long-term success. Pretending they can actually effect change in your life is a waste of time. That type of goal-setting leaves you making the same New Year's resolutions year after year. I've been accused in the past of being a little harsh—okay, sometimes a lot harsh—but the question you must ask yourself is, "Do I want to rattle off random and generic goals just to make small talk, or do I want to set goals I can actually achieve and use to change my life?" If you chose the latter, then keep reading.

HOW TO SET FINANCIAL GOALS YOU CAN ACHIEVE:

1. **BE SPECIFIC.** So you want to improve your credit, save money, and pay off bills? Great! Join the club. What do you really want to achieve though? Undefined goals are nothing more than dream killers. In order to achieve financial goals you must be deliberate about your intentions by using concrete numbers to gauge your success. Write down the goal, and be clear about dollar amounts, percentages, dates for accomplishment, etc.

    For example:
    GOAL 1: I will improve my median credit score by forty points by June 1, 2013.
    GOAL 2: I will add $1200 to my opportunity fund by December 31, 2013.
    GOAL 3: I will pay off $2120 of debt and eliminate one credit card and three medical bills by December 31, 2013.

2. **BE DELIBERATE.** So you have great quantitative goals now, but how will you really reach them? It's always easier to divide a large task into smaller steps to avoid becoming overwhelmed. To achieve your goals, get in the habit of creating "Next Steps" on a quarterly, monthly, or even weekly basis, depending upon your goal. As you begin to cross action items off your smaller list, continue to add additional steps until your goal is reached.

    For example:
    GOAL 1: Request a copy of my annual credit report by January 10th.
    GOAL 2: Identify three places on my budget where I can save a combined $100 per month by February 15th.
    GOAL 3: Call creditors and negotiate more favorable interest rates or repayment terms by February 1st.

3. **BE ACCOUNTABLE.** You've got your big goals all worked out, and you even have action steps to keep you moving along, but if you don't achieve your goals, who will know anyway? Well, that's where accountability comes in to play. Accountability is probably the single greatest motivator for achieving your dreams. Most people won't share their dreams with anyone for fear of failing in front of friends and family. If no one knows you had a goal, then no one will know that you failed, right? Unfortunately, that's the worst attitude to have. It may sound cliché, but to be successful, you need the support and encouragement of someone in your life. Whether it's a dear friend or close family member, share your dreams with someone you can trust, and let them help you help yourself.

WHY SHOULD I CARE ABOUT WHAT'S GOING ON IN THE ECONOMY?

Many people live as if the economy within their own home is independent of the nation's economic trials or triumphs. Unfortunately, this simply isn't true. You must stay aware of what goes on in the real world, because it has a huge impact on your personal life. This isn't to say that if the national economy is in a slump, you'll have to be, but it may affect job opportunities that you're banking on or change how your investments perform.

One of the beauties of being financially sound is the ability to weather the ups and downs of the national economy. Being prepared to mitigate national financial woes is one of the benefits of planning, saving, and investing. Unlike a staggering number of Americans, you'll be able to withstand the storm, because you already live beneath your means, debt-free, and with plenty of money in savings to support yourself should you encounter job loss or any other financially devastating occurrence.

I started my first business at twenty-one years old when the real estate market was booming. Experts had long forewarned that the housing bubble may burst, but the money kept rolling in, and being young and naïve, I refused to heed economists' reports. When it was all said and done, the bubble did burst, and a lot of us in the industry were left soaking wet! I wish I would've gotten out earlier, but at least I had savings for that very rainy season.

WHAT OTHER RESOURCES SHOULD I USE TO GET CONTROL OF MY FINANCES?

I wholeheartedly suggest reading material from a diverse group of personal finance authors and bloggers until you find methods and styles of planning, saving, and investing that work with you and for you, and which coincide with your values. There's no one way to do anything in life. The goal is just that you take action and do something! I've been reading about this stuff for years and there's not a single interpretation I agree with 100%. Take what works for you, and feel free to leave behind the parts that don't.

A few of my recommendations are listed here, because I know how quickly we all want our information these days. You'll find a complete list in Appendix A.

BOOKS WORTH READING:

Secrets of the Millionaire Mind	T. Harv Eker
A Purse of Your Own	Deborah Owens
Girl, Get Your Money Straight!	Glinda Bridgforth
Live It, Love It, Earn It	Marianna Olszewski
Prince Charming Isn't Coming	Barbara Stanny
Smart Women Finish Rich	David Bach
Women & Money	Suze Orman

BLOGS TO SUBSCRIBE TO:

RealMoneyAnswers.com (Of course, a shameless plug!)
BargainBabe.com
BudgetsAreSexy.com
DailyWorth.com
FinanciallyWiseWomen.com
GirlsJustWannaHaveFunds.com
GetRichSlowly.org
LadiesWhoLaunch.com
LearnVest.com
MoneyCrashers.com
TheSimpleDollar.com
WiseBread.com

EARN MORE MONEY

You were born as the solution to someone else's problem. Your true job is to find the prosperity that rests in first finding your purpose.

AFTER TRAVELING ALL OVER the country and meeting women from all walks of life, I've come to recognize a key point that many personal finance gurus seem to have all too conveniently forgotten. Women earn less money over the course of a lifetime, but we're often the primary providers for children, as well as family elders. It's not enough to tell women to use a budget and act as if all their financial woes will magically melt away. While some of us may not formally budget, when you're caring for three to five people on a limited salary, you typically know where *every* dollar is going. The problem isn't necessarily mismanagement of funds. Sometimes the issue at hand is less about outgo and more about income. How can you maintain all of the obligations you've taken on and still pursue the opportunities that will literally change the entire course of your family's destiny and legacy?

The recipe for financial success is simple: the highest income you can achieve coupled with the lowest expenses you can maintain for your personal standard or quality of life. When I speak about earning more money, most people assume I'm only encouraging entrepreneurship. As an aspiring entrepreneur since the second grade and an official entrepreneur since founding and managing a boutique real estate, mortgage, investment, and escrow brokerage at just twenty-one years old, it's no secret that I believe in using your gifts and strengths to create income. All right, so I do push

AFFIRM

I admire wealthy and successful people.

entrepreneurship quite a bit, but I also believe you can grow where you're planted. Women are shattering glass ceilings in Fortune 500 boardrooms across industries, and the progress of our gender as a whole depends on the success of these ladies. As a matter of fact, I take my hat off to them and know that I am who I am because of the pathways and trails they continue to blaze.

Whether it's in your business or someone else's, there are lessons to be learned and a purpose to be fulfilled. Deuteronomy 8:18 of the Old Testament teaches us God is the one who gives us the ability to produce wealth and that means He's also given us all we need to earn more money. We just need to identify those gifts and use them strategically.

WORKPLACE WISDOM

TIMES HAVE CERTAINLY CHANGED over the last few decades. Many women have traded in neatly pressed aprons and sparkling kitchen utensils for overstuffed briefcases and fully loaded laptops. The impact women have made on the modern workplace is undeniable. From C-suite executives all over corporate America to CEOs of Fortune 100 companies, women are on a mission to run the world. Awesome indeed, but for one small problem. We still tend to be the minority in these positions, and many of us remain clueless about what it truly takes to make it to the next level in our organizations and industries, and unfortunately it shows.

When you come from an environment where the main purpose of work is to survive, and not necessarily thrive or grow professionally, you may feel slightly behind the curve. Because of this, many women are completely unfamiliar with what it takes to secure the employment we want, set and achieve long-term career goals, and ultimately pave the way for a successful and fulfilling life, as well as a comfortable retirement.

While you may struggle from time to time with navigating the unspoken rules of the business world, there's still much you can do to empower yourself and improve your position. It simply requires learning and implementing a little workplace wisdom.

WHY HAVEN'T I FOUND MY DREAM JOB?

It's extremely hard to find something when you're not exactly sure what you're seeking. Maybe you're used to rattling off a list of things you hate or would like to change about your current employment, but have you taken time to sit down and imagine what your dream job would entail? It could be right under your nose in your current company. Or your dream may not even exist in your industry, which means you need to start looking elsewhere. Listen. Even if you earn more money doing what you do now, if you aren't happy or fulfilled, you'll just find a way to blow it and mismanage what you have.

You have a right to do work that you love. In our society, we seem to think that privilege is reserved for a select few: athletes, entertainers, and über-wealthy business people. Aren't you tired of hearing how *they're* living the life of their dreams, when you can't say the same thing yet? Don't you deserve to have the same kind of happiness and fulfillment?

Whether you work on your own or for someone else, it's imperative that you engage in work you love. Once you gain clarity around what you actually want in your dream job, you can create the space to receive what you desire. That's not to say what you want will magically appear, but now you can become intentional with your speech and strategic with the activities you engage in and the people with whom you choose to associate.

Take a moment to find clarity by answering these questions.

- *What do I really want to do? (What do I do best with the least amount of effort? What brings me joy? What would I do daily, if money were not a factor?)*
- *Who do I really want to work with as clients and/or co-workers?*
- *What types of activities will I be responsible for on a day-to-day basis?*
- *Where will I work? (home office, executive office, Starbucks)*
- *What will my work schedule look like? (days off, hours per day, etc.)*

Draft a description of your dream job.

_____

_____

_____

_____

_____

_____

If what you've described is at all possible in your current work environment, complete this section. If you're convinced that the job you want is completely impossible to find in your current work environment, skip to: *How do I know when it's time to find new employment?*

WHAT CAN I DO TO GET NOTICED FOR THE JOB I WANT?

Figuring out how to climb the ladder within your company is no easy task. You've been busting your butt doing good work, but still don't understand why you're getting passed over for the promotions for which you're clearly qualified. Well, let's talk about what you can start doing immediately to get noticed and prevent another opportunity from passing you by!

1. **GET CLEAR ABOUT YOUR TRUE VALUE.** This is not about what you "feel" like you contribute to the team. You need to identify your contributions and be able to quantify them at a moment's notice. Know current statistics on your work. Measure your successes in terms of cost savings, increased productivity, and overall contribution to the company. Did you save your department $34,000 this quarter? Are you already at 96% of your annual goal? No team wants to lose their most valuable player, and similarly no company wants to lose their most talented employee. Be crystal clear, first with yourself and then with the powers that be, about what qualities you bring to the table.

    Real TALK

    Cut the emotion and quantify your professional value to make a case for promotion. Your boss doesn't care what you "feel" like.

2. **SHARE YOUR DESIRE TO MOVE UP WITH YOUR BOSS.** Learn how to articulate your wishes effectively. Unless your supervisor or manager is a mind reader, don't assume they know you're interested in another position. They might believe you're 100% comfortable doing what you've been doing all this time, especially when you're so darn good at it! Ask for a face-to-face meeting rather than attempting to present your case in a letter or via e-mail. That type of one-way communication doesn't allow you to develop a mutual understanding of the situation and what to do about it. Ask about opportunities for advancement that may be coming up, and find out how you can prepare to take advantage of them. Try to

enroll your boss in your vision and use the meeting to toot your own horn a little by sharing the running list of professional accomplishments you compiled while getting clear about your value.

3. **BEGIN TO LOOK THE PART.** A mentor shared with me years ago that you dress for the job you want, *not* for the job you have. This doesn't mean you should spend extra money on clothes you simply cannot afford, but it does mean you should do the best you can with what you have. Try not wearing jeans and sneaks just because your office is laid-back. Do you want to blend in with your co-workers or wear a sleek pair of slacks and pumps, so you stand a little above the rest?

> ✅**AFFIRM**
>
> I work because I want to work, not because I have to work.

4. **NETWORK ON THE JOB.** Remember, moving ahead isn't only about who you know. It's also about who knows you! Don't reserve all of your networking skills for those awkward business networking mixers at the club. Get to know different folks in and outside of your department. Make a friend in the HR department. Aren't they usually the first to learn of internal job postings? If another department piques your interest, seek out information about what's going on and how things work there. Let the department's manager know you'd be interested in learning more and would even be willing to come in after hours or on an off day to help out. As long as it doesn't affect your performance in your current position, your manager shouldn't be upset, and you'll let everyone know you're definitely the one to watch for the next big opening.

Most people sit around complaining and waiting to be noticed. Be willing to go beyond what the average person is willing to do, and expect the best. Get clear, get vocal, get connected, and get noticed for the job you want!

HOW DO I NEGOTIATE A HIGHER SALARY?

Earning more money may not mean an entrepreneurial effort for you. It might be as simple and strategic as negotiating a raise on your current job. Before you can do that though, let's be clear. The typical employee only works hard enough so they don't get fired, and their boss pays them just enough so they don't quit. If you're on your second warning for coming into the office late, submitting incomplete work, or anything you know in your soul is workplace suicide, and you're still there merely by God's grace, this information won't help you. If you've been on your game, ask yourself these questions in order to prepare for your next salary negotiation.

Real TALK
If you only work hard enough to avoid getting fired, you're in no position to ask for a raise.

1. **WHY NOW?** In order to create a good game plan, you have to understand the *why* behind what you're doing, or your efforts will be scattered and emotional. Ask yourself plenty of questions to get to the root of why you want, need, and deserve a raise or promotion. The fact that you're behind on bills could be a motivation for you, but that won't be enough to sway your superiors. Is there a position coming available for which you truly qualify? Are you hoping you can have a position created based on extra duties you're already performing?

2. **WHY AM I VALUABLE?** You've been patted on the back and told you were great in the past, but have you really kept a running list of your own accomplishments? If not, it's time to start a "brag folder." Keep all positive reviews, notes of appreciation, thank you cards, and the like together in a place you can access immediately. Your goal is to become crystal clear about what qualities you bring to the table, so you can learn to articulate them effectively. You don't want to appear bratty or cocky, but you do want to make sure that you're not ashamed to toot your own horn when and where it's appropriate.

   Know current statistics on your work. Quantify your successes in terms of cost savings, increased productivity, and overall contribution to the company. Never just say you hit your annual goals back in September. Make sure everyone knows that to date, you're at 125% of your goal and counting. Now that's value, especially when others are struggling to hit 70%! It's also a lot more professional than saying, "I do more work than so-and-so."

3. **WHERE'S MY RESEARCH?** You have to know as much as you can about the pay scale of the company, as well as that of the industry. Check out sites

like www.salary.com or www.payscale.com, which collect salary and career data from millions of people across thousands of industries to give you accurate salary averages narrowed down to your metropolitan area. If you're maxed out for your job, then the reality is that it may be time to go after another position. If you haven't hit the ceiling, then you're stockpiling serious ammunition!

4. **WHO SHOULD I TALK TO?** In some workplace environments, where there's only one manager or you report directly to the owner of the business, this is pretty obvious. Other companies are layered with an over-whelming chain of command. While you might think it makes sense to go straight to your supervisor, remember that although they may adore you, they likely don't control the budget.

It could very well make sense to speak with your Human Resources department first to assess what your options are. They might be able to give you helpful tips on what they've seen take place in order for salary increases or promotions to be given. Now remember, this is not an op-portunity to go and complain about how overworked and underpaid you are. As much as HR is a department that's supposed to maintain confidentiality, the reality is that people talk. Don't let something neg-ative get back to your manager before you have a chance to present your thorough and well researched case.

5. **WHAT SHOULD I OFFER?** Oh, you thought you could ask for something without offering to give something? Not quite. Giving you additional income means that the bottom line for the business will receive less income. If you've been denied an increase in the past, maybe the numbers just didn't make sense. If you go in ready to declare how to make this a win-win situation, you may actually have a shot. The most positive way to approach a request for a raise is to ask for extra work and responsibility. You can link this to a pay increase, if not immedi-ately, then in the future. This is an approach that employers respond to better than simply asking for more pay for doing the exact same job. Additionally, you might want to ask for a performance related bonus or increase, subject to generating more output than current or expected levels.

AFFIRM

I boldly walk through life displaying confidence.

6. **HOW AND WHEN SHOULD I ASK?** Ask for a face-to-face meeting rather than attempting to present your case in a letter or via e-mail. Either of these is just a one-way communication and won't allow you to develop a mutual understanding of the situation and what to do about it. It can also be perceived as a demand, no matter how politely you feel you worded it. After all, written content is always left up to the perception of the reader, not necessarily the intent of the writer.

If you have a review coming up, you can wait until then, but if not, simply ask your boss for a review meeting to discuss a personal matter. Never say, "I want to talk to you about a raise." No one will be clearing their calendar for that conversation. In the meeting ask what opportunities for advancement may be coming up and how you can to prepare to take advantage of them. Ask what flexibilities exist and what the standard is for setting and increasing pay levels. Who does your boss have to make a case to? Will he/she support you? What would improve your case? What commitments would the company want from you? What you can put in and what can be given in return? Approach the process positively and constructively, and remember that it's a discussion, not a demand.

If you're unhappy with your salary, and you feel underpaid or undervalued, you'll do your reputation and future a lot of good by approaching the matter in a professional, well-prepared, and objective way.

WHAT DOES MY PERSONAL LIFE HAVE TO DO WITH MY PROFESSIONAL LIFE?

We can't help it. Whether we hear Apple, BMW, Coca-Cola or Wal-Mart, we automatically create very specific images in our head about each one of those brands and what they represent to us. Likewise, very specific images come up when we hear names like Beyoncé, Cher, or Michael Jackson. Brands don't only pertain to businesses, but to people, as well. It's important to understand that whether you're trying to or not, *you* represent a brand. Whether you want to accept it or not, there's absolutely no way to separate your personal and professional brands. Just think of

Real TALK

Your personal and professional brands are inseparable. Just ask any celebrity.

the late Whitney Houston or athlete Michael Vick. What they may have considered "personal business" still managed to impede their professional brands. While some can bounce back, many never do.

Let's tackle three areas where your personal life impacts your professional brand.

1. **YOUR APPEARANCE AND ATTIRE.** What does your appearance say about you? Remember that getting up and getting dressed isn't just reserved for the days you go into the office. In today's society, any place in which you set foot has the potential to produce an ideal client, business partnership, or new contract. Do you enter each day expecting opportunities to come your way? If so, there's no such thing as just "running out." You never know who you might run into. You may not always be aware of it, but there's always someone watching you who has the potential to bless you.

   I teach personal finance classes weekly, and it's impossible for me to remember every face in a room of dozens and sometimes hundreds of people. But it never fails. I run into former students at Target, furniture stores, nail salons, and even the airport! I doubt a single one can say I've had to apologize or make an excuse for my appearance.

2. **YOUR SOCIAL MEDIA PROFILES.** What do your tweets, pictures, and status updates say about you? If you're an attorney, but every picture of you on social media portrays you as a drunken party animal, how seriously do you expect potential clients to take you? People who may want to do business with you are searching far beyond your LinkedIn profile. Yes, we see your crisp collared shirt and blazer on LinkedIn, and yes, you've managed to scrape together a pretty impressive paragraph or two about your experience, but consumers are smarter these days. We know the truth about you exists in your late night tweets and the Facebook albums you refuse to restrict to friends and family. As far as we're concerned, that's the *real* you. At the end of the day, potential clients and employers alike want to do business with you, not your LinkedIn representative!

Real TALK

Potential clients and employers will check out your social media activity. Be careful what you post or tweet.

3. **YOUR ASSOCIATES AND EXTRACURRICULAR ACTIVITIES.** What do your friends say about you? Again, accept it or not, your network determines your net worth. Period. When you're out and about, who do people see you hanging out with? Whatever perception others have of your associates, they may begin to have of you. Like grandma always said, "Birds of a feather flock together." If you're investing a lot of time in folks that aren't going where you desire to go, then you're wasting a lot of time and setting yourself back.

Make sure you're seen at networking events relevant to your industry. Invest your time in people and activities that support your dreams and goals and put you in front of and around people who have brands that can lend credibility to the brand you're developing.

Building your personal and professional brand takes time, a little maintenance, and enough self-control to resist showing off your best mid-drift shots on Facebook. Regardless of the sacrifice, brand development is a part of the process that prepares you for your destiny and sets you up to earn a few extra dollars. Now what's more exciting than that?

HOW DO I AVOID WORKPLACE DRAMA?

It's rather unfortunate that this topic has to be discussed, but I've been around long enough to know that it's 100% worth the mention. I want to specifically answer this question, because so many well-meaning women fail to see how their involvement in workplace drama hinders their professional progress, and ultimately has a negative impact on their financial well-being. While many women acknowledge the existence of workplace drama, very few will acknowledge their role in perpetuating it.

This kind of drama comes in many forms, but when you break it down into the simplest terms, there are only two types of drama in the workplace. There's the drama you actually cause, and there's the drama that you may not have started, but somehow became involved in.

Here are a few things to keep in mind as you bow out of the office mess in a graceful and professional manner.

1. **PINPOINT THE SOURCES OF DRAMA QUICKLY.** There's a common confusion about the difference between drama and everyday professional challenges.

In order to overcome the negative effects of drama, you need to understand what it looks like. Generally speaking, anything that involves gossiping, instigating, stealing or undermining someone else's work, or an extreme display of emotions, such as crying, is considered drama. Issues such as tight deadlines, healthy competitiveness, or commitment to policies and procedures, whether you like and/or agree with them or not, are *not* workplace drama.

Take a moment to assess all the circumstances before you today. Categorize which issues are truly instances of drama and which may simply be related to the natural culture of your organization.

2. **ACKNOWLEDGE YOUR ROLE IN THE DRAMA.** Think back to when and how the drama began and what you may have said or done to contribute to the problem. Whether you were the initiator or welcomed the initiator's invitation, there's one thing we know for certain: creating change in your life must begin first with acknowledging your part. Actions and behavior can never be reconditioned without first being recognized. Unless you're willing to acknowledge your place in the drama, you'll continue to play the victim role, and the script in your mind will read like you have absolutely no control in the situation, when in all actuality you do!

3. **IDENTIFY SUPPORTING CAST MEMBERS.** Going out on a limb, I'm going to assume you're not just in conflict with yourself. Whether the supporting cast is full of people who encourage your position or those of an opposing team, there are sure to be others participating in some way in your unfolding drama. Know who the players are and how they've contributed to the scenario, and/or how they're impacted. While you can't force anyone else to change, you should at least be aware of the full picture. Whether you were the primary source of the drama or not, determining who else is actually involved may dictate how you can or should move forward.

4. **WRITE A NEW SCRIPT.** Once you can clearly identify the drama you're in and fess up to any part you've had in creating or maintaining it, you need to make a deliberate effort to change how the plot unfolds. Make a choice to remove yourself from all negative conversation surrounding

the topic, both in and outside of your work environment. What you verbalize you magnify and magnetize in your own life. If you're ready to let the drama go, you've got to be ready to let the discussion go.

Separate yourself from the people who have no desire to lead a drama-free life. You may have to collaborate on team projects, but you don't have to hang out at happy hour. Remember the point of eliminating the drama is to allow yourself to focus on what's important: building your career so you can earn more money and live the life you desire. This isn't about who's right or wrong or what other people will think of your sudden change. After all, the best dramas typically include great twists along the way, right? To place yourself in a positive light again, you'll have to remove yourself from any lurking negativity and hope that your behavior will inspire others to do the same.

REFLECT | What steps will you take to separate yourself from any workplace drama stopping you from making the progress you deserve?

ISN'T IT TRUE THAT MEAN GIRLS MAKE MORE MONEY?

Shortly after studies revealed that "pretty people" made $230,000 more over a lifetime, based solely upon appearance and not experience, another study was released asserting that people who are ruder also make more. This second study's findings are pretty clear. Researchers examined "agreeableness" using self-reported survey data and found that ruder women earned about 5%, or $1,828, more per year than their agreeable counterparts.

Does this mean we should all go to work and tell our bosses what we really think about our jobs? Eh, probably not. I can't vouch for the notion that becoming a b---- in the workplace will automatically guarantee you earn more money, but I think it's important to at least know what the study meant by "agreeableness." The authors are careful to explain what exactly constitutes "disagreeable." Rather than a raving psychopath causing all types of workplace drama, a disagreeable person is "more likely . . . to behave disagreeably in certain

UN REAL

Women who are "ruder" in the workplace earn about 5% more than their peers.

situations by, for instance, aggressively advocating for their position during conflicts."

With that being said, you have to wonder if a woman's aggressive or assertive manner may be taken for rudeness. This so-called mean girl may actually be a superb negotiator who doesn't take no for an answer. Maybe she's detail-oriented and doesn't waste time on fluff. In either scenario, wouldn't you expect a woman with these characteristics to eventually make more money?

Nevertheless, here are a few tips I think we should all keep in mind as we strive to earn that extra 5% and beyond.

1. **PROVIDE OUTSTANDING WORK.** Always present work that you can be proud of and stand behind 100%. At the end of the day, I'd like to think most people will still value work ethic no matter how cute or "disagreeable" you might, or might not, be.

2. **BE LIKEABLE.** People do business with folks they like, so let's not go overboard on the bitchiness. One of the best lessons I learned from my mother is that you really do catch more flies with honey. As a business woman, I'm well aware of the fact that one of my best traits is my aggressiveness. It's one of the reasons my real estate business was able to flourish so quickly. But I also learned early on how to manage relationships. You can get what you need from people without belittling, back-biting, and being totally obnoxious.

3. **VOICE YOUR OPINION CONSTRUCTIVELY.** Be passionate, not emotional. When you believe the team should go in a certain direction, research the facts, include your insight, and state your case in a well thought out manner. If the team decides to go in another direction, accept it and know that you gave it your all. If you did your best to voice your opinion, there's no need to pout about it. And if it turns out you were right, everyone will remember that and hopefully seek out your wisdom next time.

4. **STAND UP FOR YOURSELF.** Sometimes you have to take a stand instead of trying to keep the peace. You may be able to display leadership skills that no one knew you had, which can pay off professionally and monetarily.

5. **KEEP LEARNING AND INVESTING IN YOUR PROFESSIONAL DEVELOPMENT.** It's almost impossible to not earn more as you learn more and, most importantly, put what you learn into practice. There's just a certain confidence that comes with knowing that you know what you know! That doesn't mean you're not teachable or coachable, but rather that you're not ashamed of the investment you've made in yourself. After all, the point in learning is to share what you know to positively impact both your personal performance and the bottom line of your organization.

6. **CREATE YOUR OWN PERSONAL STANDARD FOR SUCCESS.** When you set self-imposed goals, you're not as worried about acting on every new study published. Know who you are, and be consistently confident in what you bring to the table.

HOW DO I KNOW WHEN IT'S TIME TO FIND NEW EMPLOYMENT?

If we're totally honest, you really don't need me or anyone else to tell you when it's time to move on from a job. You've known it in your gut for some time now. And guess what? According to several studies, you're not alone. Apparently, only 19% of American workers say they're actually satisfied with their job. The majority are serious when they say they're only working to get a check, and you may feel the same way.

Let's see how the following questions resonate with you.

UN REAL

Less than 25% of American workers say they're satisfied with their jobs.

- *Were you passed over for yet another promotion only to watch someone with less seniority, talent, and commitment slide into the position?*
- *Do you wake up excited to go make a difference on your job or dreading the fact that it's yet another work day?*

- *Is there a pep in your step as you move toward your office building, or do you have to sit in your car each morning and get yourself together before you're ready to get to work?*
- *Do you start the week celebrating Monday or looking forward to Friday?*
- *Do you spend a majority of your time with loved ones whining and complaining about "those people" at your job?*
- *Do you find yourself daydreaming in meetings and having to ask people what you missed?*
- *Do you get physically ill and mentally exhausted from the mere mention of your job or anyone associated with it?*

Did any of those ring a bell, even a little? I know they did for me at a very early point in my career. I'd approach the freeway exit near my office, and my stomach would tie up in knots. I'd park and cry hysterically for ten minutes while my mother prayed for me over the cell phone waves. From the time I walked in the office each day, I'd dream of what I would do when I could break away around five o'clock. And during lunch time, I'd go somewhere and shop just because. Yup, emotional spending at its finest!

After several months of this, my cousin, a single mom in her late twenties, died of a heart attack. After going to a job she absolutely hated for nearly five years, my family was convinced it was stress-induced. Talk about a wake-up call. That week, I realized I could not and would not live my life that way. I also recognized that I wasn't too young to suffer the same fate. Less than forty-five days later, I left my position and haven't looked back since, not even when the owner threatened to physically harm me and swore I'd never be successful on my own.

Am I saying you should run out and quit your job in six weeks or less? Of course not. I'd taken baby steps with my planning, but losing my cousin made me kick things into high gear, and quickly. You need to do whatever it takes to create the job environment that will keep you fulfilled.

(See: *Why haven't I found my dream job?*)

GET YOUR HUSTLE ON!

MANY WOMEN COME TO me feeling overwhelmed, overworked, underpaid, and unfulfilled. The typical e-mail I get from a prospective client confirms that she's tired of giving her all to employers that don't value or care about her, or who don't have the means or desire to pay her what she's worth. Sound familiar?

For some women, entrepreneurship is a lifelong dream, but for others the desire to launch their own business may stem from getting fed up with all things workplace associated. Either way, there's usually one slight problem. When your personal finances are in disarray, it becomes very hard to take that leap of faith, a situation which often leaves women stuck in dead-end jobs. To make matters worse, we tend to create our own imaginary bubble of worry and fear, which paralyzes us and prevents us from taking even the first steps toward going solo. In the words of Martin Luther King, Jr., "Faith is taking the first step even when you can't see the whole staircase."

Luckily, with today's technology and the vast resources available, it doesn't have to be an either/or discussion. If you're not ready to leave your job, don't! That doesn't mean, however, that you can't start preparing. It's possible to keep your job, create a master plan, and get your hustle on all at the same time. So let's go!

HOW COULD I POSSIBLY START A BUSINESS AND KEEP WORKING?

Every day I coach women who are waiting for more time, waiting for children to grow up, waiting to get married, or waiting for some person, place,

Starting a business while you work your job, allows you to test the waters while you're still getting a paycheck.

or thing outside of themselves to bring their dreams to fruition. When I ask why not go after their dreams *now*, the number one answer is that they work full-time.

Well, I guess this depends on how you look at things. It's the glass half full or half empty scenario. Maybe your job is in the way *or* maybe it could be a blessing to test out the viability of a new business while you have the consistency of a steady job. In the book, *Hustle While You Work*, the author, Hotep, asserts that "Your job is not an obstacle in the way of your entrepreneurial dream; your job is THE WAY to your entrepreneurial dream." There's something we don't hear too often.

I'm a firm believer that had we all been taught how to hustle *while* we worked, the economy may have suffered the same major setbacks, but many of us would've weathered those setbacks a lot better. Far more people could have sustained mortgages, car notes, and college tuition a little longer had their dependence not been on a single stream of income. Maybe if we were taught more about creating passive income (income that does not come from active participation in a business) instead of believing we could still simply "go to college and get a job," we'd be much further along as a country.

In addition to already having a full-time job, there are several other common excuses many people give as to why they can't hustle while they work. Make sure you're not letting these excuses hold you back.

1. **I DON'T HAVE TIME.** Did anyone ever break up with you because they had a problem with how you spend your time? If they did, the conversation might start out with, "You make time for the things you want to make time for." Yes, when you really want to make something happen, you *make* time. You don't *find* time, as if it were hiding around a corner or under a mattress somewhere. Most of us could make time if we'd turn off *The Real Housewives of* (fill in your favorite city), limit our Facebook

and internet surfing, and stop wasting time complaining and whining about all the stuff we wish we had time to do.

If you get focused and organize and prioritize your daily activities, you can easily begin to hustle while you work!

2. **ALL THE GOOD IDEAS ARE GONE.** Simply put, I'm not buying it. I'm a firm believer that we're all born to fulfill some purpose in life. We each are blessed with unique gifts, talents, and abilities to bring to the marketplace. No one is saying your big idea has to be the next Facebook. It's possible to create additional income and live a fulfilling life doing something that's already been done. Whether it's already been done or not, if it's never been done by you, then there's still an opportunity. Don't quit before you start.

Assess your gifts, talents, and skills, and figure out a way to put your own unique spin on them, so you can begin to hustle while you work.

3. **I'M JUST NOT READY.** Here we go again with the waiting. What are you waiting for now? Perfect timing? Progress beats perfection any day. At some point, you just need to start wherever you are. Even if it's on a very small scale, you'll be allowing the momentum to build while perfecting your product or service. No matter how many books and blogs you read, or how many informational interviews you do, there will always be something else you simply don't know yet. If I worried about completely understanding blog monetization before I started my blog, you wouldn't be reading this book right now.

> **Real TALK**
> When it comes to building a business, progress beats perfection any day.

Pool all of the information and resources you have under your belt, and just get started! When you do your part, trust me, God or the Universe or whoever you recognize as your higher source, will bring forth everything else you need. It all starts with YOU!

If nothing else, I hope recent economic instability has reminded you that your path to financial independence and a secure future lies within your own abilities. If you have a job, be grateful that you do, because many people don't. But don't use it as an excuse. Use it as a stepping stone, and hustle while you work.

> **REFLECT** | What excuses have you used to delay moving forward with your business idea? Do you recognize now why those really are just excuses?

HOW AM I SUPPOSED TO BALANCE A JOB, A SIDE-BUSINESS, AND A FAMILY?

Well, I hate to be the bearer of bad news, but women all over this country do it every day. I was one of them for nearly two years, so you won't get much sympathy from me. A majority of the book you have in your hands right now, and my last book, *Real Money Answers: College Life & Beyond*, were both written while I worked full-time at a non-profit agency counseling hundreds of men and women on credit and money management. I was also keeping up my blog, writing for magazines, coaching women privately, and managing the hectic schedules of my traveling husband and a small child with more activities than the average adult!

Do many people consider that type of schedule crazy? Absolutely. What you have to ask yourself is whether or not you want the results and approval of the average person. You must also ask if you want the results of the successful people who have come before you. It all boils down to what your priorities are. When something is important to you, you make time to do it. It just so happens in my case I loved my job, because it was truly a dream job for me. I'm also extremely passionate about my business, and the well-being of my family is of the utmost importance to me. At the time, there was no room to say no or to slack off in any of these areas.

Contrary to popular belief, I actually did sleep, and eat, and even have fun occasionally. The truth is I did what I learned to do while maintaining a hectic schedule and going to college. I prioritized.

I have everything I need to get where I'm going.

Understanding how to truly prioritize is the key to balancing everything your heart desires. Can it be hectic and crazy at times? Absolutely.

But I don't believe you have to short-change any area of life, as long as you're disciplined.

Here are a few ways you can create discipline and balance in your life.

1. **KEEP A WRITTEN CALENDAR OR APPOINTMENT BOOK.** As our dependency on smartphones and tablets grows, we ignore the importance of writing activities down and being able to physically see our week at a glance. Writing information down allows us to remember the people and things to which we've obligated ourselves and to identify the gaps where time for our business or social activities can be added.

2. **START ASSIGNMENTS IN ADVANCE.** If you always stay ahead of the game on your work, you never have to worry about other parts of your life interfering with last minute assignments. If you have orders to fill, or in my world, deadlines for article submissions, always stay one week ahead. Even if you have to cram in some work time, the less you have to do twenty-four to forty-eight hours before the due date, the better.

3. **ORGANIZE EVERY PART OF YOUR LIFE.** The more organized you are, the better. It helps keep you sane and keeps your family safe from the crazy woman you probably become when you can't find something. Trust me. I know all too well!

The average person wastes 153 days of his or her lifetime looking for misplaced items.

Here are a few things I do to organize and add structure to my life.

1. **USE BLOCK SCHEDULING.** This means only doing certain work-related activities at certain times or on certain days. For example, Mondays are my writing days. I don't coach or take meetings or work on business development. All I do is write. It helps me stay focused and productive, as opposed to jumping around from project to project. You may want to decide that you only return emails or phone calls at certain times throughout the day. This will help you regain control of your schedule.

2. **TEACH KIDS TO PREPARE IN ADVANCE.** I used to believe my daughter deserved the same freedom I have to choose an outfit at the start of each day. I

soon realized that was absolutely, positively the worst idea in the world. It was too time-consuming. Instead we decided her clothes for the week should all be ironed and laid out on Sunday nights. Lunches and snacks get packed the night before each school day.

3. **PUT EVERYTHING IN THE SAME PLACE EVERY TIME.** According to a 2012 study, we spend a total of 3,680 hours, or 153 days, over our lifetime looking for misplaced stuff. Just think. That's nearly two years of forty-hour work weeks, which could be invested directly into your new business just by keeping things in order.

4. **LEARN TO SAY *NO* MORE OFTEN.** There's so much going on in life that pressure from friends, family, or co-workers can make you feel like you're either obligated to do things or that you're missing out on something. Your priority of creating the life you want has to outweigh the comments and opinions of others, who may not agree with or understand your vision. Sure, you'll have to sacrifice a little now to get where you want to go later. If your dreams are big enough, isn't the sacrifice worth it?

HOW DO I EVEN KNOW WHAT I'M GOOD AT?

In my *Mindset + Money Master Class*®, I teach women how to discover what they're good at by helping them understand their Sweet Spot. Now, before you go getting any ideas, let me explain. The Sweet Spot is simply the intersection between your gifts and skills and what the marketplace will actually pay you for possessing those qualities and packaging them properly.

Your Sweet Spot is the intersection between your gifts and skills and what the market will pay you for them.

The first step in recognizing your Sweet Spot is to assess gifts and talents.

Answer the following questions.

What do you do better than anyone else around you with the least amount of effort?

_____

_____

_____

_____

On what subjects are people constantly asking you for advice?

_____

_____

_____

_____

What service or product are you constantly giving away for free, even though you know it has value?

_____

_____

_____

_____

What gives you energy?

_____

_____

_____

_____

What are you happiest doing? With whom? When?

_____

_____

_____

_____

HOW CAN I BEGIN MAKING MONEY FROM MY HOBBY?

Every change starts in the mind. Every change starts with a decision. You first have to decide that you'll stop calling your gifts and talents "hobbies,"

Visit sites like sba.gov or score.org to find free business plan templates.

if you truly desire to make money using them. It's time for your thinking to shift, just as your conversations will have to shift. You'll no longer be the person who fixes everything for free or the one who can do this or that for "whatever you want to give me."

From the most specialized service to the simplest task, there's someone out there that needs what you have to offer. They just have to know you're ready, willing, and able to do it. No matter how small or large your business idea, you'll need to write out a plan, because if you fail to plan, you're planning to fail. Utilize sites like www.sba.gov or www.score.org to help you fill in the template for an official business plan, but don't be overwhelmed by the process.

Fill in the answers below, along with the gift assessment in the previous section (*How do I know what I'm good at?*), and get to the fundamentals of how to profit from your hobby. Momentum is a beautiful thing. Just start.

IDENTIFY YOUR SKILL SET.
What degrees or certifications have you earned? They don't have to be directly connected to your passion or hobby.

_____

_____

_____

_____

What work experience do you have? What volunteer experience have you had?

_____

_____

_____

_____

How is your experience relevant to your gifts in any way? This is your opportunity to think outside the box. I once saw a billboard for a dancing dentist. She created her unique position in the marketplace by saying she was graceful on her feet and with her hands. Say what you want, but it set her apart from the pack, and it was interesting.

_____

_____

_____

_____

UNDERSTAND THE MARKETPLACE AND YOUR MARKETING.

You can have the best idea in the world, but if no one knows you or your idea exists, you'll never get off the ground. In addition, if your target audience doesn't know you're speaking directly to them, you're finished before you start.

Who specifically makes up the market for your product or service? Just saying it's for women isn't enough. A woman of what age, income, religion, and marital status? Does she have children? A college degree? Go deep, and get specific.

_____

_____

_____

_____

Where are these women? What types of places do they frequent? How do they typically receive information? List at least seven low-cost methods you can use to get your message to your ideal customer. (a blog, Facebook, Twitter, an ezine or newsletter, etc.)

_____

_____

_____

_____

WHAT IF I'M JUST NOT THE "SALESY" TYPE?

The great part about connecting with your purpose and creating a business with your natural gift is that you're never selling anything. Look at it as simply sharing your gift with the world. When you believe you're doing what you were born to do, passion and enthusiasm almost seem to ooze out of your pores. Your ears perk up at the mere mention of anything related to your field, and your eyes light up with a spark of infectious enthusiasm. It's so much a part of who you are, you begin to naturally talk about it or get drawn into conversations on the topic.

Real MONEY

When you're passionate about sharing your gifts through your business, you never have to worry about selling.

Your primary job, beyond perfecting your skills, is to train yourself to talk about them in a clear and concise way that says, "I'm ready and open for business." What you've probably done in the past, like many of us, is brush off your skill or expertise as no big deal and allow others to pick up on your passion and enthusiasm, only to abuse it by paying you little to nothing.

To take the focus off selling yourself and closing the deal, try the following strategies.

1. **FOCUS ON RELATIONSHIPS.** When you focus on really getting to know potential clients, you give them an opportunity to decide for themselves that they want to work with you. You've likely heard, "People do business with people they like." Depending on your product or service, you may need to factor a "getting to know you" period into your engagement of potential customers. While building their trust, you're also finding ways to stay in front of them and ensure that when they are in the market for your product or services, they immediately think to patronize you.

2. **BECOME THE EXPERT.** Really work to become known for one specific product, service, or niche. When you do too many other things, people get confused and become unclear about how much you really know about what you're sharing. And when people don't trust your expertise, they instantly perceive you as someone who's just trying to sell them something.

3. **PORTRAY YOUR BRAND IN A CONSISTENT AND PROFESSIONAL MANNER.** Should your ideal client be in the market for what you have to offer, they'll come to

you believing it's their privilege and honor to work with you, as opposed to you having to prove yourself to new people over and over again.

4. **THINK LIKE A MARKETER.** When you swap hats and think like a marketer, you can start to identify pockets of potential for your business. Once you know where your ideal customer is, what she eats, what she drives, what she wears, and many other details about her, you find opportunities to get in front of her and share your gift. If you've done it correctly, people will naturally be attracted to you.

WHAT CAN I DO TO MARKET MY BUSINESS?

You may feel like you don't have the time, money, or energy to market your new business venture, and that's understandable. The reality is, however, that you really have to make time for it. Speaking from experience, I can say with certainty that marketing my business and brand this time around has been significantly simpler and less expensive than it was ten years ago when building my real estate firm.

Here are just a few steps that will serve you well in building your brand. (If you don't believe me, the proof is in the fact that you're reading this very page today!)

Real TALK

Success isn't just a result of who you know; even more, it's a result of who knows you.

1. **NETWORK RELENTLESSLY.** While you work to build your business, you have to remember that your success is in the numbers. Success is not 100% about who you know. It's more about who knows you. The more people who know you exist, the better. When you network at free and low-cost events, it's not just to sell someone on your product or service. You're looking to build relationships with any and everyone, from potential clients and joint venture partners to those with complementary services and sponsors or investors. (See: *How do I network effectively?*)

2. **BUILD SOCIAL MEDIA PRESENCE.** Whether you like it or not, social media is a must-have for every new or growing business, especially since it's absolutely free. If you've been resistant to change, I understand. I was, too. You're reading the words of a woman who refused an email address

in high school, because I thought it was a fad! Well, email didn't go away and neither will social media, so throw it in the marketing mix. Consistent engagement is the key to using social media to benefit your business. Brainstorming a cute Twitter handle and snagging a Facebook fan page won't be enough. Use that virtual space to speak to your target customers and prove to them through useful information that you really do know what you're talking about.

3. **BLOG ABOUT YOUR SUBJECT MATTER.** Along with building your social media presence, you'll want some place to send new fans for more information about you. A blog is a great free way to showcase your knowledge and build trust with your ideal clientele. Whether you write short posts, like I did when I began blogging in 2009, or highlight pictures of your work, use the blog to play up your strengths. Like social media, your blog needs to stay fresh and updated. Don't be intimidated by bloggers who write several posts a day. Those guys are likely being paid by a sponsor to generate so much material. You may want to grow to that level at some point, but it's not necessary when you're a newbie working to discover your voice and your niche. Don't be afraid to share relevant content from other parts of the web. If you don't have any new ideas at the moment, use someone else's. Just be sure to give them credit and post a link back to their site. Your followers will appreciate that you're scouting out great information for them.

4. **FIND JOINT VENTURE PARTNERS.** In point number one of this section, I suggest networking to find joint venture partners. What you're looking for is someone who offers a product or service which complements your own. Whether live or via the internet, you two could hold events which highlight both businesses and expose each of you to the other's audience. Never fear that involving another business or brand will take business away from you. That type of thinking will prevent your business from blossoming. Remember the Universe is full of limitless abundance. This is an opportunity for you to reach people who otherwise may never know your name.

WHAT ARE THE BASIC BUSINESS LESSONS I SHOULD KNOW?

You can never know everything, which I suppose is a lesson within itself. Entrepreneurship on any level is a journey, one that teaches you through trial and error as you go. Below I've highlighted a few key concepts every woman should be introduced to, if she plans to succeed in business. Some I've learned through my own hiccups along the way, and others I've thankfully picked up from personal mentors and by reading about and watching some of the most influential people of our day.

1. **FOCUS ON ONE THING.** As I've said, we're all blessed with unique gifts, talents, and abilities. You may be blessed with ten, but you can't focus on all ten at the same time and either expect success or expect us to buy you as the master of all things. You have to be okay with narrowing your focus in the hopes that you can master one thing and become

If you claim to be the expert on everything from relationships to real estate, no one will take you seriously.

wildly successful with that first. Your goal can still be to ultimately allow that one thing to become a feeder for future opportunities.

Let's be real. No one trusts the woman whose business card states that she's a match-making relationship coach who sells real estate and braids hair on the weekends. Even if you can do all of those things, choose what you want to be known for and roll with it. Let all of your other hidden talents come out once a relationship is built, rather than squeezing them all on your business card. We, the general public, won't take you or your business sensibilities seriously, if you claim to be the expert on disparate things.

2. **BUILD STRONG RELATIONSHIPS.** Success in business is based on the relationships you build not just with clientele, but staff, partners, referrals, and really anyone you come into contact with. No matter where I am, I greet everyone with a smile. I'm nice to people. If they have a name tag on, I honor them by saying their name and holding even a 10-second conversation, which is more than the average person takes time to give.

Someone with the power to bless you is always watching what you do.

Someone told me once, that there's always someone watching you with the power to bless you. But will they want to if you're walking around with furrowed brows and a frown most the time? Will they want to when you can't even say good morning to the receptionist or janitor and obviously only speak to people who you know or who you believe can do something for you? I can't tell you how many times I'm asked to speak somewhere and walk in to find people are rude or ignore me completely. Once I'm introduced as the speaker of the evening, as a person of influence, or as someone connected to others of influence, they all of a sudden want to become best friends. Of course, in my book, the opportunity for that connection has passed and will likely not come back, even if the tone has changed within a matter of minutes. First impressions are still lasting ones.

3. **LEARN THE GIFT OF GOOD-BYE.** Know upfront that people will come and go on your journey to success, and that's as it should be. Media mogul Tyler Perry calls them boosters. These people are there to help get your rocket off the ground. Once you've launched, it may be time for a few folk to fall off. Everyone can't handle where God is taking you, and that's okay. You just have to be willing to accept that some people come into our lives for a reason and a season. When their time is up, be content with letting them go. If they're leaving to pursue their own thing, let them go and wish them the best of luck. If you have to kick them to the curb for being underhanded, let them go and wish them the best of luck. Either way, understand the gift of good-bye, and just let them go. Business will thrive once you do.

4. **INVEST IN YOURSELF BEFORE YOU EXPECT OTHERS TO INVEST IN YOU.** You can't worry about finding investors or trying to gain access to capital until you've done all you can to invest in your business. Do the hard work. Sacrifice. Build your list of fans and potential customers. Create a prototype of your product. Launch your website. Survey potential clients. Don't expect someone else to invest money in your business until you've done all you can to get the ball rolling.

5. **ONLY TAKE CRITICISM IF IT COMES WITH A SOLUTION.** A friend of mine shared a quote with me some years ago. "Effective people starve problems and

feed solutions." Everyone has an opinion. Some say they're like . . . well, you know what they say. Not everyone will buy into your vision, and you have to discern what comments or criticisms are worth your time and consideration. I'm not suggesting that you not be teachable or coachable—everyone should be. But I've learned from my own experience that if someone only chooses to point out flaws and failures, without providing examples of how I can fix the problem, then they're not really trying to help me.

HOW CAN I NETWORK EFFECTIVELY?

Your network determines your net worth. Who you will be in five years is directly related to the people you associate with now. Read any book on success and you'll find a common theme. They all stress the importance of leveraging relationships. Working in teams is an absolute necessity, while attempting to work in solitude is seen as absolutely ludicrous. You need other people, preferably people that are either smarter than you or have more experience than you in some area of life or business.

AFFIRM

I surround myself with intelligent and successful people.

If you've ever been to a networking event, you've probably run into a few of the obvious ineffective networkers. Sorry to say it, but you may be one of them, just like I used to be. You know the woman who runs from person to person shoving her business card into everyone's hand? She barely stops to build a genuine connection with anyone, but feels accomplished at the end of the night when she has twenty-five fewer cards in her designer card holder. Or maybe you recognize the wall-flower who expects everyone to find her in the corner and strike up a conversation. She's the type who will typically hold you hostage with long-winded conversation in hopes that you'll attract others. Or how about the gal who forgets that although this networking event is taking place during a happy hour on Friday night, this is not the place to shake a tail feather one minute and then try to act sophisticated the next. Any of those sound familiar?

Networking is essential to growing your business, brand, and life. Use these tips to get it done effectively.

1. **BE PREPARED.** Attending a networking event with no business cards is a rookie mistake. If you're going to jump in, do it wholeheartedly. While the most important thing is showing up, you want to show up as a professional ready for business. When you meet your ideal client, partner, or sponsor, what do you think their perception of you will be if you're unprepared? You wouldn't want them to assume that you handle business with the same lack of preparedness.

2. **SET GOALS BEFORE YOU WALK IN.** You must know what you're looking for before you even enter the event. Are you job hunting? Are you looking for partnerships, clients, or investors? How about a professional in a complementary industry? Of course, you should stay open to all kinds of possibilities, but there's nothing wrong with knowing what you want beforehand. Then you can make sure that your conversations are focused and intentional, which is important when time is limited.

3. **ARRIVE ON TIME.** Most networking opportunities take place first thing in the morning, during lunch hour, or immediately after work. Think about these timeframes. Most people will have to rush off some place and won't have time to linger. Either they're scurrying to work in the morning, back to work in the afternoon, or home to care for families in the evening. If you want to have the greatest chance to meet the most people, you need to be there during the peak time, which is the one hour smack dab in the middle. But come earlier if you want to take advantage of free food. No one wants to get to know you while you're stuffing your face!

4. **GET YOUR ELEVATOR SPEECH TIGHT.** Be able to intelligently articulate what you do and who you do it for in ninety seconds or less. If you've been talking for two or three minutes about what you do, you're probably well into ramble mode, and you may have lost the interest of whoever is listening. Write down a few different versions of your elevator speech, practice them in the mirror, and memorize them.

> **$ Real MONEY**
> Be ready to articulate what you do and who you do it for in ninety seconds or less.

5. **WORK THE CROWD.** This is probably the one that women struggle with the most. Once we find people we like, we can ride out the entire night with them and feel über-successful at the end of the event. But by not mingling, you'll miss the opportunity to meet many more wonderful people and to make important contacts. Some networking pros suggest that you spend no more than six to eight minutes with a person. This is enough time to determine whether there's a connection and to be polite when ending the conversation. Time yourself and be ready to offer a pleasant exit, such as "Pleasure meeting you, but I have to make my rounds. I will email you by X."

6. **KEEP THINGS PROFESSIONAL.** Regardless of where the event is held, remember this is business. You may be in a club setting with alcohol flowing, but don't let it confuse your sensibilities. Any event branded as "networking" should be considered just that. This isn't about socializing, and it certainly isn't the time for you to pick up anyone or be picked up by anyone. As a matter of fact, I'd have some questions about a guy hitting on you at a networking event. If something does blossom between you, won't you wonder what's really going on when he's out networking every week? But I digress. At the end of the day, no suggestive dancing, foul language of any kind, excessive drinking, or provocative dressing, unless there's something else you're trying to sell.

7. **FOLLOW UP QUICKLY.** You can follow each of the previous steps to a tee, but know that the introduction is just that, an introduction. If you don't work on building the relationship within three days of making the acquaintance, the likelihood that you'll be able to create something lasting tends to decrease drastically. You may not want to have a follow-up meeting with every person you met, but at least connect with these people on LinkedIn, a social media network for professionals. If you have a well-manicured page, this will give them an opportunity to learn more about you than you could have expressed in six to eight minutes. Look for your top three contacts from the event and send a genuine email that suggests some type of further communication within the next two weeks. Build a relationship, keeping in mind that people do business with people they like.

YOU ARE YOUR BEST INVESTMENT

CONTINUALLY WORKING ON YOUR education and personal development is not about spending more money. It's about investing in both your mental growth and future income. Continuous learning is a wealthy habit. What wealthy people recognize is that our careers, businesses, and personal endeavors cannot possibly grow when we settle in a fixed mindset that limits our thinking and requires us to rely solely on status, ego, or past experience in a world continuously faced with new innovations and new challenges. When you fail to nurture your mindset and skill set in order to embrace these challenges, you accept failure before the opportunity to succeed ever presents itself.

Whether it's the books you buy, the seminars, conferences, and trainings you choose to attend, or even the coaches or mentors you hire, education and personal advancement on any and every level is the secret weapon of the wealthy, powerful, and successful. In the words of Jim Rohn, a self-made millionaire famous for sharing his own rags to riches story, "Formal education will make you a living; self-education will make you a fortune."

Rarely is business success attributed to never having failed or to having the good fortune to avoid setbacks. Quite the contrary. A common theme you'll find from studying the courageous men and women who've triumphed in the business world is that their investment in self-education ensured that, no matter what happened, they always had the attitude and

AFFIRM

I benefit often from
seeking wise counsel.

mindset to stand back up, dust themselves off, and create their empires again. You must understand beyond a shadow of a doubt that what you nurture grows. The investment you make in your personal growth and development is the one thing that no unfortunate circumstance or ill-intentioned person can ever take away from you. You are your best investment!

HOW CAN I AFFORD PERSONAL DEVELOPMENT WHEN I'M BROKE?

Personal development comes in many forms. Your willingness to seek it out depends, like anything else, on whether you truly see it as an investment in your future or not. Those who practice un-wealthy habits will rarely see a workshop, seminar, or online coaching series as such, but they'll jump at an opportunity to wield the term "investment" when it comes to depreciating items like a classic little black dress or a name brand television. In essence, un-wealthy people tend to view objects as investments. Successful people invest in continuous learning. They know that no matter what risks they take, if they lose it all, no one can steal their knowledge. The question isn't really *if* you can afford to invest in personal development. The question is how can you afford not to?

Don't be limited by believing all personal development requires you to shell out thousands of dollars. There are hundreds of programs that offer no-cost and low-cost education in the areas of financial literacy, small business development, the arts, and much more. This journey is about the mindset. When you approach personal development as though everything

Real MONEY

Investment in
education and
personal development
is the secret weapon of
the wealthy, powerful,
and successful.

costs too much, or there aren't any programs out there, then you're absolutely right. It is too expensive, and there aren't any good programs out there for *you*. Meanwhile, someone who fits your exact profile in your very own city is taking advantage of all types of programming that will help her get her life on track. Everything begins with a decision. You, and only you, have the power to decide whether your glass will be half empty or half full.

If your glass is, in fact, half full, follow these low-cost or no-cost tips to get started on your personal development path today.

1. **GET YOUR MIND RIGHT, AND START WHERE YOU ARE.** Once you've wrapped your mind around the fact that you can and should move forward on this path, identify what area of life you want to improve first and commit to starting where you are. Your first target area may be finances, business, relationships, health, spirituality, parenting, or any number of subjects. The beauty is that as you continue to seek out opportunities for growth, the Universe will continue to bring forth amazing opportunities, as well. Just commit to beginning today.

2. **READ FOR AN HOUR OR MORE PER DAY.** A 2012 study by the Nielsen Company found that the average American household spends over five hours per day watching television. This translates to nine years of life that the average person will spend sitting in front of a box. Imagine how much further along you'll be than the average person if you make a conscious decision to use some of that time to read, rather than allowing your brain to slip into a near comatose state for hours each day.

UN REAL

The average American spends over five hours per day watching TV--time that could be spent learning.

3. **INCORPORATE LEARNING INTO YOUR NORMAL ROUTINE.** Check out books on audio from the local library or download a few on your mobile device. You can listen while getting dressed in the morning, cleaning the house, working out at the gym, or on the go. Some of my clients use their long commutes driving to work or riding on the train as an opportunity for school on wheels. Instead of wasting time on Facebook while you're waiting for an appointment, carry something you can pull out and read. The point is to make this a part of your lifestyle, as opposed to declaring you don't have time to read.

4. **TAKE ADVANTAGE OF FREE OPPORTUNITIES TO LEARN.** Don't ignore every late-night infomercial. Some offer tickets to complimentary half-day seminars. Don't go with the attitude that someone wants to sell you something. While you may be 110% right, you set the rules for how

that game is played in your world. Go with the understanding that you want to learn at least one new concept, as well as have an opportunity to network with new people. If you're truly not interested, don't feel pressured to buy anything. Simply take your notes home, determine what you can and cannot use, implement immediately, and move on.

5. **FIND A MENTOR.** Your success in any area of life is strongly determined by the people you surround yourself with. Not only do you require the support and encouragement of others to make meaningful progress, but you'll often find yourself leaning on them for advice, as well. My personal rule of thumb in this area is to not take advice from someone who is not where I want to be or has never been where I'm going. Look to mentors who are willing to be transparent about their triumphs and failures to help you navigate your course just a little better.

I'VE TRIED LOTS OF SELF-HELP SYSTEMS. WHY HASN'T ANYTHING WORKED?

As a person who offers self-help programs, I'll be the first to tell you that I don't find anything healthy or cost-effective about being a self-help junkie. When people ask me what the difference is between other personal finance authorities and me, I describe the qualities or characteristics that I believe are different, but then I politely ask them to go back and work through whatever system they've already started. We all have a common goal of helping people lead financially fit lives, and we essentially teach variations of the same information. Who you choose to work with really comes down to a personal preference.

Many people hop around from program to program and system to system searching for the magic bullet that's going to change their lives in seven days or less. I'm honestly amazed at how many people will spend ten, twenty, or thirty years running their finances into the ground and then come to me for coaching and expect to see miraculous improvement overnight. It's like people who try a six-month weight loss system and quit after three days if they haven't dropped ten pounds.

In truth, many people aren't willing to fully implement the programs they invest in. Typically, the creator of a program lays out the material in a specific way in order to give you the blueprint for how they achieved success in a certain area or how they've helped clients succeed. You can choose the bits and pieces that you really need and ignore areas that perhaps don't pertain to you, but you cannot ignore the entire system and then say the program doesn't work.

AFFIRM

I always have time to learn new wealth principles.

The disclaimers on fitness or business infomercials usually state that the testimonials are from real people, but they're not average results. You know why? It's not because the system or program fails most people. It's because we all know the average person isn't willing to do the work, no matter how much they claim they want the results.

To make progress using any system you've purchased in the last few years, I encourage you to go back through the steps and commit to intense and focused implementation for a designated thoughtful, reasonable period of time. If the instructions are to give it ninety days, be willing to invest ninety days before taking to online reviews to bash the system. If you can't make the commitment, just accept that the program hasn't worked because you haven't been willing to work it.

WHAT'S THE DIFFERENCE BETWEEN A MENTOR AND A COACH?

Coaching and mentoring are both excellent resources to fuel your personal development, but many times the terms get confused. You need to understand the difference between the two in order to decide which is right for you as you strive to achieve your professional aspirations and take your career to the next level. *Your Career, Your Way!*, by Lisa Quast, does an excellent job of explaining the difference.

"**MENTORS:** Generally someone farther up the career ladder than you, someone you admire for their professionalism, for their knowledge and for their ability to succeed in difficult situations. They are politically savvy in business and are admired for their fair treatment of others.

A mentor provides career guidance and can help with career opportunities because they are generally a senior-level manager from within the same company or industry. They act as your advisor and provide suggestions and guidance on development opportunities, career paths, and leadership strategies. A mentor relationship may be formal (arranged between the individuals or with the help of the HR department) or informal. A critical element within a mentoring relationship is mutual respect. A mentor is generally not paid for services.

COACHES: A coach focuses specifically on your personal development and learning. Coaches observe your performance, analyze your skills, behavior and attitude and provide you with an unbiased, outside perspective to help you improve your efficiency and effectiveness. A coach may be a manager or colleague within your company or industry; however, a coach is most commonly someone who is hired by you or hired through your human resources department for a contracted length of time (usually six months to three years) for a specific fee. The coach works with you during the contracted time period on such areas as knowledge transfer/training, behavior modification, behavior modeling, and image enhancement. They may help you develop or enhance a skill set and improve leadership capabilities.

A coach is hired to help you become the best you can be both personally and professionally; in essence, a tutor. Hiring a coach is usually a formal process in which the coach and "coachee" agree upon specific coaching goals, discuss and agree on expectations of the relationship (such as confidentiality and safety), agree on how they will communicate and schedule meetings (over the telephone, in person, via email, etc.), agree on how they will measure success and the specific metrics that will be used, agree on the time commitment for the coaching sessions, etc. In a coaching relationship, it is critical for you to be open to having your coach observe your work and for you to be open to feedback."

SHOULD I GO BACK TO SCHOOL IF I ALREADY HAVE DEBT?

Since the Great Recession started in 2008, I've counseled many people who used our weakened economy as an opportunity to go back to school and secure advanced degrees. At first mention, I can see why someone may think this is a viable route to take her to the next level of career success during difficult economic times. But after seeing the results for many who chose this route without a well thought-out plan, I can honestly say this method isn't for everyone. As a matter of fact, I'd go so far as to say many people could reach the next level in their careers by simply investing more time in their basic personal development and implementing what they've already learned.

If you plan to go back to school, be clear about your objectives and the odds of those things materializing. For example, I've met people who took out $80,000 to earn an MBA, but, years after completion, aren't making any more money than they were before the decision to get the additional degree. Adding additional letters behind your name or seeing your name embossed in gold on a fancy certificate may feel great, but having to pay back tens of thousands in loans won't feel so good if you're not earning significantly more money.

If your current employer offers some type of higher education incentive, then by all means, take advantage of it, if you're convinced that getting the additional degree will make the impact you want. As with any other endeavor, the ultimate results are based upon how much work you're willing to put in after the classes have ended. Beware of the bucket list mentality. "I'm just doing it because I've always wanted to," isn't a good reason to go deeply into debt. While I'm a fan of accomplishing whatever you set your mind to, I'm not a fan of adding additional debt to your life simply because it somehow makes you happy. If you have to take on debt to be happy, I'd suggest a new pair of shoes or some bag you've been eyeing. The thought of that kind of frivolous spending doesn't excite me, but we could surely figure out a plan to pay that off a lot sooner than more student loan debt!

Are there instances when going back to school, with or without taking on debt, has helped someone advance personally and professionally? Of course. I'd be foolish to claim otherwise. But I find that those people usually create a solid plan before embarking upon the educational journey. They've researched, spoken to mentors, found the cheapest route to accomplish their goal, and planned what they'll do with the new knowledge. More than likely, these are people who haven't decided to go back to school simply to live off of a refund check, which sadly happens quite frequently. They've put in the work to make it work and obtain the results many hope for, but few achieve.

UNREAL

The average cost of graduate school at a public university is $30,000 per year and rising.

IS IT POSSIBLE TO AVOID STUDENT LOANS IF I GO BACK TO SCHOOL?

As an adult in the real world, you've learned by now that the notion of going to school, taking out more loans than you can afford, and banking on getting a high-paying job at the end of it all is completely delusional. With living expenses, the average cost of a graduate program at a public university is about $30,000 per year and rising, with private colleges costing about 30% more. Undergraduate tuition isn't far behind. With this in mind, you should definitely be concerned about what it will take to make it through with minimal debt and the smallest amount of money out-of-pocket.

It's definitely possible to avoid student loans, whether your desire is to complete your undergraduate degree or return as a graduate student. No different than the advice given to high school students and their parents, it all comes down to whether or not you plan properly and plan well enough in advance.

Here are a few ways you can avoid student loans.

1. **EXPLORE SCHOLARSHIPS, FELLOWSHIPS, AND ASSISTANTSHIPS.** Undergraduate schools generally have a central financial aid office, where you can get information about aid for any degree program. In many graduate programs, aid is given out by academic departments or the specific graduate school instead of the central financial aid office. That means you should search for a graduate admissions official or someone affiliated with the program to help you sort through available options. Scholarships are based on merit, talent, and/or need and can be awarded by schools or private organizations. Fellowships are given to pay for research or education, and requirements will vary. Assistantship is just a fancy term that means you're paid to be a professor's assistant.

2. **ENTICE SCHOOLS TO COMPETE FOR YOU.** If you happened to be a top student in your undergraduate studies, apply to several graduate schools and let them know you're searching for the best financial aid package. They might compete with a strong offer in order to convince you to choose their school.

3. **GET YOUR CURRENT EMPLOYER TO PAY.** Approximately 50% of U.S. companies have some type of tuition assistance program in place. Many

companies looking to boost their collective skill set, without hiring new people and spending resources on training, will sponsor all or part of an employee's graduate schooling through tuition reimbursement. If your company doesn't, talk with the human resources department about how a master's degree or Ph.D. would benefit both

Real MONEY
About 50% of U.S. companies offer some type of tuition assistance to employees.

you and the company. You'll want to play up the connection between your coursework and your job description. Just know that having your education paid for by your employer might mean committing to work for the company for a set period after you complete the degree or program. If you leave the company early, you may have to pay back part of the tuition.

4. **RESEARCH POTENTIAL TAX BENEFITS.** There are three different ways to take advantage of tax benefits for graduate school: the Lifetime Learning Tax Credit, tuition expense deductions, and student loan interest deductions.

   Ask your tax professional to make sure you take advantage of these methods which allows individuals to subtract thousands of dollars annually from their tax bill.

5. **TALK TO YOUR UNDERGRADUATE SCHOOL.** If they have a graduate program, many schools will offer a tuition discount to alumni. This is especially true if you left with great undergraduate grades and can snag a few recommendation letters from respected professors who are still there.

WHAT'S THE REAL DIFFERENCE BETWEEN GRANTS AND SCHOLARSHIPS?

Both grants and scholarships can be used to fund a college education. Unlike loans, their recipients are not required to repay the money upon graduation or at any point in the future. While neither has to be repaid, there are a number of key differences between the two.

GRANTS: A grant is money given by a non-profit organization that will generally be tax-exempt, as long as all of the money is used specifically for tuition, fees, books and required course-related supplies. One of the best examples of this type of organization is the government. Corporations and foundations may also provide grants to students. Grants will often be given for a project, and the student will be expected to report information about the project to the donor. Grants vary widely in their requirements, amounts, and expectations. They may be awarded to people other than college students, including small business owners or entrepreneurs.

SCHOLARSHIPS: A scholarship is a form of financial aid specifically geared toward students who are attending college. It's used to finance their education, and it may pay a part of their tuition or cover all related expenses. Scholarship recipients need to meet certain requirements, both before and after they've obtained the award. Most of these scholarships will require students to maintain a minimum GPA, and may also require them to take a certain number of credits each semester. Scholarships may also be based on gender, major, race, place of origin, relationship to an organization, or any other criteria stipulated by the donor.

To research the differences even further and get more information on where to start your search, check out www.educationgrant.com. You'll also find other options for paying for college, like work-study programs and military benefits. Sources of money you don't have to repay should be your primary options when you're looking for financial aid. Loans should be an absolute last resort.

WHAT SHOULD I DO WITH A FINANCIAL AID REFUND CHECK?

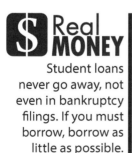

Student loans never go away, not even in bankruptcy filings. If you must borrow, borrow as little as possible.

Typically, if you receive financial aid for an amount more than what your school requires in tuition, housing, and other fees, you'll receive some type of refund check. One of the largest financial blunders both undergraduate and graduate students make is assuming that it makes sense to take that refund and live now on money that will cost so much more later.

If the refund check is only from scholarships and grants, or other money that does not have to be repaid, you can keep the money and use it to help with your expenses. Be aware, however, that any amount in excess of specific tuition-related fees will be subject to income tax.

If you received a loan in your aid package, please realize that this is still money you have borrowed. If money is not being gifted or granted to you, you will be responsible for paying back every dime, plus interest. College loans never go away. They must be paid back one way or another. They can't even be included in bankruptcy filings, should you be forced to use that option one day.

If you must borrow, you should borrow the smallest amount of money necessary. Depending on the hope that you'll come out of school with a six-figure job that will erase all debt is naïve and foolish. Student refund checks are issued at the beginning of every semester, so remember to review the list below each semester to make sure you are making wise decisions.

1. **BORROW ONLY WHAT YOU NEED, ONLY WHEN YOU NEED IT.** The amount you borrow is far less than what you'll have to repay. By the time you finish paying off your student loans, you'll probably end up paying around 30% more than the amount you borrowed, depending on how many years you take to pay the loans off and at what interest rate. Imagine borrowing $30,000, but having to repay well more than $40,000 when you only needed $20,000 to begin with! If you don't properly plan, your student loan payments may be much larger than you expected and take a bigger chunk out of your future paycheck than you're prepared to pay.

UNREAL

By the time you pay off your student loans, you'll likely end up paying around 30% more than you borrowed.

2. **WHEN CALCULATING HOW MUCH STUDENT LOAN MONEY YOU'LL NEED, ASK YOURSELF THESE QUESTIONS.** Can I reduce my expenses? (The answer is almost always yes.) Have I exhausted options for free money first? (See: *Is it possible to avoid student loans if I go back to school?*)

3. **USE YOUR STUDENT LOAN MONEY TO FINANCE YOUR EDUCATION, NOT YOUR LIFESTYLE.** If you're going to borrow money, use it only for tuition, books, and related

fees. Keep it separate from whatever money you use to pay rent, purchase groceries, or do any of the other things an adult is expected to do. Why? Unless someone else is footing your entire bill, every dollar you spend unnecessarily will be a dollar you'll have to borrow now, which means another dollar *plus interest* you'll have to repay later.

Allow any excess to be applied to the following semester or contact your student loan lending institution to find out how you can send it back. You may not get the shopping spree you want now, but think of the lifestyle you can live later, while your friends are spending every penny they make to repay student loans.

If you MUST get a student loan refund (as a realist, I recognize many of you will do so), at least budget it in a way that will set you up to win in the long term.

- **STEP ONE:** Budget your refund. You're going to need to decide at the outset how much of your money you can allocate to expenses each month, and make sure your total expenses are less than your refund. Be realistic and write down every single thing, no matter how large or small you think it is.

- **STEP TWO:** Place the bulk of your money in a high-interest savings account. An online bank like Capital One 360, formerly known as ING Direct, is a great option. The fact that it takes about forty-eight hours to transfer funds can help prevent you from spending impulsively.

HOW CAN I TAKE ADVANTAGE OF LOAN FORGIVENESS?

Loan forgiveness is one of the only ways you can pay off a student loan without using money; instead you pay with service. The government takes care of a portion of your debt for you if you agree to put in some time serving your country. While there are loan forgiveness opportunities for specific disciplines, such as law or medical school, the most common programs revolve around volunteering or working in areas of high need.

Here are a few examples of loan forgiveness opportunities.

1. **AMERICORPS.** If you're willing to devote a year of your life to volunteering for AmeriCorps, an organization dedicated to addressing the most critical needs of local communities, you'll be rewarded with $5,550 to spend on your qualified college debts and possibly a stipend of up to $10,900. For more information, visit www.americorps.gov or call 800-942-2677.

   ## Real MONEY

   With loan forgiveness, the government pays a portion of your debt in exchange for your service to your country.

2. **PEACE CORPS.** If you want to see the world and pay off debt, go traveling with the Peace Corps to a foreign country and provide your volunteer service there. You'll get to defer most of your student loans until after you leave the program, and additionally, you may get some of your loans reduced by up to a staggering 70%. For more information, check out www.peacecorps.gov or call 800-424-8580.

3. **MILITARY SERVICE.** You can achieve complete loan forgiveness and stay in shape at the same time if you join the Army Reserve or the National Guard after graduation. You may receive up to $10,000 to pay off your loans.

4. **TEACH FOR AMERICA.** Entering the field of education is already a noble choice, but volunteering to be placed in the most disadvantaged schools in America is an additional challenge worthy of handsome reward. This program not only offers the option of student loan repayment, but also covers the interest on loans you have deferred during your two years in the program. Get more information at www.teachforamerica. org or call 800-832-1230.

5. **SOCIAL SERVICES.** If you're a full-time provider of early intervention services for the disabled, employee of an agency that provides services to families of low-income communities, a full-time nurse or medical technician, or full-time law enforcement or corrections officer, your loan may be eligible for complete forgiveness. Restrictions apply, but I'd say it's worth doing your research.

MANAGE MONEY WISELY

Only 20% of personal financial success is head knowledge;
the other 80% is behavior.

"IF I ONLY MADE** more money, I'd be fine." That's the classic lie people tell themselves when things aren't going well with their finances. But financial success isn't based solely on income. One of the most famous examples of doing a lot with a little is that of Canadian school-teacher Roberta Langtry, who earned a modest annual salary of no more than $30,000 for most her life. By supplementing her income with small entrepreneurial ventures, living below her means, and investing wisely, she amassed a tidy fortune. During her lifetime, she regularly donated money to people in need, and when she passed away in 2005, Ms. Langtry left $4.3 million to her favorite charity. Her story demonstrates that smart money management can make you wealthy, no matter how small or large your salary may be. Yet countless Americans earn three times what Ms. Langtry made and wind up with no financial legacy to leave behind. What's wrong with that picture?

Being a good steward over your finances means taking care of, and showing respect for, what you have now. If you can't manage $100 wisely, then why on earth would the Universe trust you with $100,000? If it did, consciously or subconsciously, you'd likely find a way to mismanage it. Don't think so? Let's ask the thousands of American lottery winners who hit rock bottom within a few years of hitting it big.

A 2010 study, entitled *The Ticket to Easy Street? The Financial Consequences of Winning the Lottery*, found that winning a lottery prize of $50,000 to $150,000 only postponed bankruptcy. It didn't prevent it. This implies that even though the median winner of a large cash prize could have paid off all of his unsecured debt or increased the equity in his new or existing assets, he did neither.

The results of the study indicate that giving $50,000 to $150,000 to a person usually won't fix their finances. While these recipients are 50% less likely than small prize winners to file for bankruptcy immediately after winning, they're *more* likely to file for bankruptcy three to five years after winning. Furthermore, bankruptcy petitions filed in the five years after winning reveal that the net assets and unsecured debt of big money winners are no different from those of small prize winners. In other words, that extra money makes no lasting difference.

When you don't possess a healthy respect for money or a desire to nurture it and grow it, you ultimately disrespect it and lose it. In order to maintain what you make over the long-term, you have to decide that you're ready to manage money wisely.

GET IT TOGETHER!

I'S EASY TO DECLARE that you want to save more, invest more, and become debt-free, but with the wrong advice and no money management system in place, even the greatest of intentions go to waste.

The first step in managing your money wisely is to show respect for the money you already have. Checking your mailbox less than once a month and leaving receipts balled up at the bottom of your purse aren't signs of respect. A sign of respect would be utilizing a money-managing method that's easy for you to maintain, an organized system rather than a shoebox under your bed. De-cluttering and organizing financial records is actually my favorite exercise to do when I'm coaching or consulting women on personal finance. It's my first opportunity to not only remove the physical clutter we can see piling up, but to also clear away the mental clutter that consumes their ability to manage money effectively. After all, it's difficult to get your financial life in order when your financial documents are completely out of order!

It's equally difficult to get your finances in order when you're getting no financial advice at all, or even worse, bad advice from others who aren't well versed in the subject. With a few simple steps, you can finally get it together by building a financial team and implementing a system, both of which will support you as you strive to reach your goals.

WHAT DOCUMENTS SHOULD EVERY WOMAN HAVE ON HAND?

It's easy to think of financial documents as nothing more than a few utility statements and sales receipts, but for a complete picture, you'll need to pull together much more. So get what you can find out of shoeboxes, off your kitchen counter, out of junk drawers or the little envelopes with months printed on them, or wherever you've been cramming all the bills, check stubs, and other stuff you swore you'd organize one day. Today's the day.

Removing the physical clutter will clear away the mental clutter and allow you to manage your money effectively.

Review the list of important documents below, gather them together, and indicate whether you (H) have the document, (N) need to obtain the document, or (X) the document doesn't apply to your household. Collect the documents you have, and request the ones you need. This process sets the foundation for you to work through the rest of this section of the book.

CHECKLIST OF IMPORTANT
LEGAL DOCUMENTS & FINANCIAL STATEMENTS

Important Legal Documents that Apply to My Family

- _____ 1. Birth Certificate(s)/Adoption Papers
- _____ 2. Marriage License
- _____ 3. Divorce Papers
- _____ 4. Social Security Card(s)
- _____ 5. Passport/Green Card(s)
- _____ 6. Naturalization Documents
- _____ 7. Will
- _____ 8. Power(s) of Attorney (Personal/Property)
- _____ 9. Mortgage or Real Estate Deeds of Trust
- _____ 10. Vehicle Registration/Ownership
- _____ 11. Other

Tax Statements

- _____ 12. Previous 3 Years' Tax Returns
- _____ 13. Property Tax Statements
- _____ 14. Personal Property Tax Statements

_____ 15. Other

Financial Accounts

_____ 16. Bank/Credit Union Statements

_____ 17. Credit/Debit Card Statements

_____ 18. Retirement Accounts (401K, TSP, IRA, etc.)

_____ 19. Investment Accounts (Stocks, Bonds, Mutual Funds, etc.)

_____ 20. Other

Sources of Income/Assets

_____ 21. Recent Pay Stubs for All Sources of Income

_____ 22. Government Benefits (Social Security, Temporary Assistance for Needy Families, Veterans', etc.)

_____ 23. Alimony Income

_____ 24. Child Support Income

_____ 25. Professional Appraisals of Personal Property

_____ 26. Rewards Accounts (Frequent Flyer Programs, Hotel Rewards, etc.)

_____ 27. Other

Financial Obligations

_____ 28. Mortgage Statements

_____ 29. Lease

_____ 30. Utility Bills (Electric, Water, Gas)

_____ 31. Car Payments

_____ 32. Student Loans

_____ 33. Alimony Payments

_____ 34. Child Support Payments

_____ 35. Elder Care Facilities

_____ 36. Other Debts

Insurance

_____ 37. Property Insurance

_____ 38. Rental Insurance

_____ 39. Auto Insurance

_____ 40. Life Insurance

_____ 41. Other

Medical

_____ 42. Health Insurance ID Card(s)

_____ 43. Record of Immunizations/Allergies

_____ 44. List of Necessary Medications

_____ 45. Disabilities Documentation

_____ 46. Living Will

_____ 47. Dental Records/Child Identity Cards/DNA records

_____ 48. Other

Military

_____ 49. Current Military ID

_____ 50. Military Discharge DD 214

_____ 51. Other

Other Financial/Legal Documentation

_____ 52. _____

_____ 53. _____

_____ 54. _____

Once you have all of these documents together, make a copy of the entire packet. As important information is often printed on the backs of these documents, please be sure to copy both sides. Store the document copies in a safe deposit box or a small waterproof and fireproof safe, which you can find at office supply stores.

*Download Operation HOPE's Emergency Financial First Aid Kit to print down the entire checklist as well as other Personal Household Information worksheets by visiting http://www.operationhope.org/emergency-kit

HOW CAN I KEEP MY FINANCES ORGANIZED?

My financial life is in order, because my financial documents are in order.

As you've learned, it's pretty tough to get your financial life in order if your financial documents are scattered across your home, office, and automobile. In the last exercise, you found all of your most important legal documents and financial statements. (See: *What documents should every woman have on hand?*) It's time to organize them in a systematic way that will save you from ever having your important information in disarray again.

WHAT'S NEEDED:
    1 Dozen Hanging File Folders
    1 Box of 25 File Folders
    1 Plastic File Tote

WHAT TO DO:

STEP ONE:
Label the first hanging file folder **"Legal Documents."** In it, place items that are imperative to keep track of, but which don't necessarily fall into a financial category. In one folder, you'll place vital records like birth certificates and adoption papers. In another, you might place your marriage license or divorce decree. Here is where you'll also file your social security card, passport, and green card or naturalization documents. Copies of wills and powers of attorney, in sealed envelopes, should also be placed here.

STEP TWO:
Label the second hanging file folder **"Tax Returns."** In it, place three file folders, one for last year, the present year, and next year. Mark the year on each folder's tab, and put into it all of that year's important tax documents, like W-2 forms or 1099s. If you can't find the documents, but used professional tax preparers in the past, call them and ask for back copies.

STEP THREE:
Label the third hanging folder **"Financial Accounts."** If you have several checking and savings accounts, create separate file folders for each of them. Keep your monthly bank statements here, as well as any ATM slips or deposit slips you retrieve during the month. (Note: If you have several accounts with no money in them, just consolidate. Don't waste time, energy, or paper.) Additionally, use this area to store information about retirement accounts (401k, TSP, IRA, etc.) and investment accounts (stocks, bonds, mutual funds, etc.).

STEP FOUR:
Label the fourth hanging folder **"Income and Assets."** Create a folder to store recent pay stubs or copies of checks received for self-employment income. Hold on to proof of all government benefits such as social security income. Use a separate folder if you receive alimony or child support.

STEP FIVE:
Label the fifth hanging folder **"Household."** If you're a homeowner, this includes mortgage statements, property tax bills, HOA documents, and other related expenses. If you're a renter, this should contain your lease, the receipt for your security deposit, renter's insurance policy, and the receipts for your rental payments. I would also include folders for electricity, gas, and cable, and other recurring household expenses. These are also statements you should keep up with regularly. My clients have caught hundreds of dollars erroneously charged on phone and cable bills by comparing multiple statements over a period of time. Don't forget to also include any agreements you have between yourself and any roommates or boarders, relationships which have become rather common since the Great Recession. No matter how close you are as friends, when money is involved, document everything!

Compare billing statements, such as cable and phone bills, over a period of time to catch any billing errors.

STEP SIX:
Label the sixth hanging folder **"Credit Card DEBT."** Make sure to capitalize the word DEBT, so it stands out and bothers you every time you see it. I'm not kidding. Create a separate file for each credit card account you have. Prayerfully, this step does not take up all your file folders. If it does, no worries. We'll handle that shortly.

STEP SEVEN:
Label the seventh hanging folder **"Loans."** Place any documents associated with your loans here. This may include student loans, car loans, personal loans, and the like. Each debt should have its own folder, so Sallie Mae has one folder, and your Chase Student loan has another. Each folder should contain the loan note, your statements, and payment records.

STEP EIGHT:
Label the eighth hanging folder **"Insurance."** It will contain separate folders for each of your insurance policies, which may include car insurance, health insurance, disability insurance, and the like. Remember your homeowner's or renter's policies should have been filed away in the Household section. If you have any other policies besides those, include them here as well.

STEP NINE:
If you have children, put together a folder labeled **"Children's Documents."** It should hold all statements and other records pertaining to any accounts they have and accounts you have for them, such as college savings. I also add a folder for child care to keep track of those expenses for tax purposes, as well as a folder with immunization records and other health-related documents needed for school.

STEP TEN:
Label the tenth hanging folder **"Personal."** It should contain files for personal expenses such as clothing, grooming, dental services, organization dues, and the like. Create a specific folder for your medical files, such as copies of your health insurance cards, statements from your physician's office or the hospital, and lists of necessary medications.

As you begin the process of putting together your system, you may find you're missing some documents. Whatever the reason you don't have them on hand, today is a new day. That was something the old you didn't keep up with, because no one taught you how much it could simplify your life. Now that you know better, put the files together as best you can, and figure out how or where to get your hands on whatever's missing. The important thing is that you've taken the first step, and that's something you should definitely be proud of!

HOW LONG SHOULD I KEEP FINANCIAL DOCUMENTS?

Managing your money can create a lot of paperwork when you're doing it consistently. Once you have your filing system in place, shred documents periodically to make sure you always have the most recent and relevant information. (See: *How can I keep my finances organized?*) Don't burden yourself by keeping these documents longer than necessary.

If you're like me and prefer to have things on hand longer, then scan the documents before you shred them. Save the scanned images in organized folders on your computer, but remember to back it up often.

If you opt for paperless or e-billing and receive your statements in your e-mail box, there's no need to scan. You can simply save each statement as a PDF. It saves time, paper, and energy, but make sure it's the right choice for you. Will you open and review the statement or bill the same way you would if it arrived on paper? It's easy to forget about bills that only exist on the Internet. Make sure it's the right option for you.

Here are some timeframes for keeping financial records.

KEEP FOR A YEAR OR LESS:
- **Monthly Bills** – Review for accuracy, but there's no need to keep them for more than a quarter at the most.
- **Credit Card Bills** – Review for any billing errors, and keep for at least six months.
- **Paycheck Stubs** – You should always have your last three pay stubs. You never know when you'll need to prove income for a loan or some other necessity. Keep the last few in the year to compare against your W-2 or 1099. If they don't match, go to your employer and request a correction. Otherwise, you can shred them. Your W-2 is sufficient for filing taxes.
- **Insurance Policies** – Always keep the most recent policy. Old ones don't matter once a new one takes effect.

KEEP FOR TWO YEARS:
- **Bank Statements** – Review when you receive them. Look for unauthorized purchases, and keep twenty-four months of statements on hand. For the self-employed, this is particularly important. In some instances, the absence of a regular W-2 and paycheck stubs means you'll need to prove your income by using bank statements.

KEEP FOR SEVEN YEARS:
- **Tax Documents** – I know seven years seems like forever, but so will an IRS audit, if you don't have your tax returns in order. If you think you're

due a larger refund, you have three years to file an amended return, and the IRS has three years to audit you, if they think you made a mistake. The IRS has six years to audit you when they think you underreported income, and there's no time limit when they believe you blatantly filed a fraudulent return.

If you've lost old tax returns and would feel better if you had a copy, contact your tax preparer, and if all else fails, request a copy of past tax returns from the IRS. You can get a tax return transcript for free in about two weeks by calling 1-800-829-1040.

KEEP FOREVER OR INDEFINITELY:

- **Loan Documents** – Keep these for the life of the loan, and destroy them once you've paid them off and have a title or other final document proving payment in full.
- **Receipts** – Keep anything documenting a major purchase, like jewelry or a computer. You never know when it might come in handy.
- **Long-term insurance policies or investment accounts** – Keep these documents until maturation of the investment.
- **Brokerage Statements** – If you've already begun investing, you'll get monthly statements telling you how much you've made each month. Keep brokerage statements until you receive the annual statement at the end of each year. Keep annual statements until you sell the invest-ment. You'll use the statements to prove your capital gains or losses when you file taxes.

WHAT SOFTWARE DO YOU SUGGEST FOR MANAGING MONEY EFFECTIVELY?

There are many money-management software options available, and I don't believe in dictating a one-size-fits-all approach. After all, we each have unique money personalities, and every day companies are creating new software to help us track and manage our money in ways that fit our individual needs. You can expect to find programs that will allow you to manage every aspect of your finances, including your accounts, bills, in-vestments, taxes, planning, and goal setting. I prefer web-based programs, because they're consistently updated. These can cost up to $19.99 per month, but you can also find free options.

The ideal personal finance software for you should be based on your personal style, give basic advice to help you make informed decisions, and provide ample user-friendly features. It should make managing your finances convenient and stress-free, identify money leaks for you, and help you make better investments and increase your personal net worth.

Here's a list of the criteria to search for when choosing personal finance software.

BANKING & BILLS
The ability to import all account data, including transactions, directly into the software is a standard tool you'll need to make wise money decisions. The best personal finance software allows you to manage your savings and checking accounts, as well as your loans, credit cards, and mortgage accounts, in one place.

PERSONAL INVESTING & GOAL SETTING
Look for personal finance software that provides its users with the tools needed to manage stocks, bonds, mutual funds, 401K accounts, and the like. Personal investment options within the software will also allow you to plan for retirement, home purchases, college expenses, debt relief, and other financial goals.

TAX OPTIONS
Some personal finance software can export all of your financial information into tax software, help you find missed deductions, and estimate your tax withholdings and capital gains.

USER FRIENDLINESS
Personal finance software must be extremely easy to use, allowing you to track transactions, set up accounts, and see detailed reports.

REPORTING
Reports are a great way to track your progress. You want to see how well, or not so well, you've done with your money management in any given period of weeks, months, or years. Typical software utilizes pie charts and line graphs to illustrate cash flow, personal investing, and all additional

transactions. The ability to see exactly where your money is going is essential when you're trying to decide where to cut back in order to save.

HELP & SUPPORT

In order for all of your questions to be answered in a timely manner, you may want to search for software that provides an online user manual, customer forum, email support system, and integrated help section.

ARCHIVING & SECURITY

Security is an extremely important feature for your personal finance software. Your account numbers, personal information, and other bank information are used to set up and manage accounts within the software for your convenience.

Having archived financial files saved and categorized is perfect for tax season, or if, by chance, you happen to be audited.

WHAT PROFESSIONALS SHOULD I HAVE ON MY FINANCIAL TEAM?

Your success, in any area of life, is strongly determined by the people with whom you surround yourself. Not only do you require the support and encouragement of others to make meaningful progress, but you'll often find yourself leaning on them for advice, as well. And as much as you may love and appreciate close friends and family, you simply can't take financial advice from everyone.

While I'm a big proponent of taking an active role in your money management, there are several pieces of the financial puzzle that require professional help. Having the right team in place can make all the difference in how you manage your finances and put your money to work for you, instead of against you. Here's a list of the small group of professionals you may need to enlist to advise you on business and personal finance decisions.

Real TALK

The right team of professionals can make sure your money is working for you, not against you.

Personal Finance Coach - I'm not starting with a personal finance coach simply to toot my own horn. Quite often I receive referrals from colleagues in other financial disciplines who wish their clients had met with someone like me first. It's very difficult for a financial planner or advisor to do their job when the client lacks basic budgeting skill, claims she can't find the money to save, and is still struggling with emotional spending due to childhood issues. These professionals want to work on more complex investment strategies and long-term planning. If you're starting from scratch and need someone to hold your hand through the process, you should start with a coach that can help you set the foundation and make life easier for the professionals up ahead.

Accountant - When life isn't too complicated, and you can file a simple return via TurboTax or one of the other tax preparation software programs, I'm not opposed to that option. But an actual accountant can do a lot more than prepare tax returns. Some will help analyze your big picture and help you set up a system for managing and reviewing your finances. They can also keep pace with life changes that affect your taxes, such as getting married or divorced, having a new child, or sending one off to college. The IRS doesn't care about what you didn't know when an audit hits, so get the advice you need upfront.

Estate-Planning Attorney - While not the most exciting thing to think about, getting things in order to care for the loved ones you'll eventually leave behind has to be at the top of your priority list. This professional will help assemble the documents necessary to ensure things go smoothly when that inevitable time comes. These documents include a will, financial and medical powers of attorney, which let others make important decisions for you when you can't make them for yourself, and in some cases, a revocable living trust, which lets your estate avoid probate. You may need other documents, dependent upon your unique scenario. You can also do all this for yourself on sites like www.legalzoom.com or www.rocketlawyer.com, but any legal documents should still be reviewed by a professional for accuracy.

> **$ Real MONEY**
> Getting your estate in order for the loved ones you'll eventually leave behind should be a top priority.

Financial Planner - A financial planner helps you create a road map for your financial future. The planner works with you to create plans for retirement, taxes, and college tuition, according to your specific needs and financial objectives for every phase of your adult life. By keeping abreast of new tax laws, current trends, and market developments, a planner works with you on a strategic level.

Financial Advisor - Financial advisors are commonly confused with financial planners. Most people use the titles interchangeably, which is very misleading. Financial advisors deal specifically with investing. Their job is to advise you on how to best invest your money in accordance with the road map you created with your financial planner. The advisor's primary function is to provide guidance. For example, an advisor might guide you in finding the most tax-effective way to save for your child's education. You can use the expertise of a financial advisor to assist primarily with market related investments. Most advisors are highly knowledgeable in the areas of mutual funds, stocks, and bonds. Some financial advisors specialize in specific investment products. There's some debate about whether it's best to go with a fee-based or a commission-based advisor. My view is that the financial advisor's integrity, expertise, and ability to work well with you are more important factors.

Mentor - No matter how old you are or what you've accomplished, everyone needs wise counsel, either from someone who has the success you desire or from someone who's been there, done that, and will be transparent enough to tell you what mistakes to avoid. Once you've surrounded yourself with a team of the best consultants, coaches, and confidants you can find, put a cherry on top and find a mentor that will help you stay clear of the costly mistakes you'll likely make if left to your own devices.

HOW DO I CHOOSE THE RIGHT PROFESSIONALS FOR MY PERSONAL FINANCE TEAM?

Knowing you need professional help is a wonderful first step, but finding a trusted team that understands your personality and objectives takes work. Admittedly, I've only learned to choose the right people through trial and error. I've lost a lot of time and money relying on information from people who simply didn't know what they were doing. I wanted to be upset. Okay, I was actually a tad past that point. You know when you're so upset you have to speak very slowly and lowly, or you'll end up saying totally inappropriate things? Yeah, I was upset like that when I got hit with a five-figure tax bill a few years back.

Real TALK

Don't waste time and money relying on advice from people who don't know what they're doing. Find an expert!

When we thought about it more deeply, however, my husband and I recognized where we went wrong. We didn't have a system for how we evaluated the people who got to be on our team. We were so busy "making moves" that we went with the first referral we received, instead of doing our due diligence. We also made the mistake of not making a change when our life circumstances grew beyond the experience and expertise of our professional. We wanted them to just learn what we needed, but you should always have someone who's an expert at what they do.

When putting together your personal finance team, don't do what I first did. Save yourself some time, money, and heartache and with these tips.

1. **EVALUATE YOUR NEEDS, STRENGTHS, AND WEAKNESSES.** While you want to keep a list of strong individuals and companies at your fingertips, you probably won't need everyone all the time. Your team might include an accountant, insurance agent, or financial planner, but you'll only call on each one when the need arises. Know your strengths, and figure out where and when you need help with your weaknesses.

2. **USE REFERRALS.** The best way to find someone reliable is to ask for recommendations from your friends, family, and colleagues who've experienced a high level of care and service and have reaped the benefits you desire. Keep in mind that you're looking for referrals from people with whom you share similar profiles. If you're renting and have no assets, it's probably not necessary to pay the fees charged by your multi-millionaire uncle's CPA just yet.

3. **ASK FOR A CONSULTATION.** I learned not to wait until the last minute to reach out to new professionals and meet with them one-on-one. Most professionals offer some type of free consultation. For whatever reason, many

people don't take them up on it. If you've taken time to evaluate your needs, you should be able to compile a list of questions you'd like to have answered. This isn't about getting free advice crammed into a twenty-minute session. This is about determining the proper fit for a long-term professional relationship.

Real MONEY

Take advantage of free consultations to ask questions and determine if each professional is the right fit for you.

4. **TRUST YOUR GUT.** Only hire people with whom you feel a connection. Ask yourself how easy it is to talk with the person. If it's easy to talk to him or her about everyday matters—family, background, the economy—you'll find it's easier to talk about business. That doesn't mean you only look for someone you like on a personal level. They still have to be qualified. (Just saying. Unfortunately, I've made that mistake, too.)

5. **FIND SOMEONE WHO THINKS AHEAD.** I've learned to hire people who think like entrepreneurs, as they should, and forecast not just for themselves, but for me. With so much going on, you don't have time for people waiting for you to tell them what to do. Besides, you probably won't even know what needs to be done next. That's why the heck you're hiring professionals! It's valuable to work with folks who can help you avoid potential pitfalls rather than people who help you recover from mistakes.

6. **DON'T FEAR CHANGE.** If a member of your financial team isn't working out, make a substitution before you lose your blouse behind their antics. You may have to try a few people before you find the right one. That's okay. As you move along and adjust your own expectations, you'll eventually find the right fit.

BUDGETING EFFECTIVELY

WE PROBABLY DON'T NEED to cover the many ineffective methods you've discovered for budgeting over the years. Your "system" has probably left you asking yourself questions like:

Didn't I just get paid? Why am I broke already?
Why is it so hard to stick to a budget?
Shouldn't I have way more money saved by now?
Did I really pay a $34 overdraft fee for a $5 purchase?

At some point, you've got to be tired of working hard, getting paid, and then looking up and wondering where all your money went. The foundation of developing good financial habits rests upon your ability to master budgeting. Before your brows furrow, remember that budgeting is about creating the vision for your money and making it plain. Budgets are simply a way to tell your money where to go, so it's working for you and not against you.

Budgets are so fundamentally important because they do more than help you prevent senseless overdraft fees. Your budget sets the tone for the rest of your financial plan. How much you can save, give, spend, invest, and pay down debt all hinges on your ability to budget effectively.

WHY DO I REALLY NEED A BUDGET?

Have you ever gotten paid on a Friday and been broke by Monday? Think that's extreme? Not if you ask 30% of the people I teach and coach. It helps to realize a budget is just a tool to help you identify where your money is going, as opposed to whining over where your money went. I love the Bible verse Habakkuk 2: 2 that says "write the vision and make it plain." Think of the budget as the vision for your money. You're plainly writing down how your money's coming in and determining how it should go out, without depending on those ridiculous running tallies in your head.

> **Real TALK**
> Your budget sets the tone for your financial plan and provides the foundation for developing wealthy habits.

Budgeting is also instrumental in determining where the holes are in your financial planning. If you want to save more, invest, or pay off debt, but can't seem to figure out how you can possibly do it all, a budget will help you find the missing money. In the *Mindset + Money Master Class*®, I show participants how finding just $50 in your budget can help cut your debt repayment time in half. I walk you through the process and give you a spreadsheet I've created so you can plug in your own numbers and see how quickly you can reach your goals.

> **Real TALK**
> You should run your household finances like a business. Make decisions based on the numbers, not on emotions.

Run your household like a business. Businesses determine when to hire, fire, and make significant purchases based on the budget. Imagine, as the CEO of your life, being able to create logical systems and take calculated steps based on the facts, not the fictional and emotional places from which many of us manage our money.

HOW DO I DIFFERENTIATE BETWEEN NEEDS AND WANTS?

This is one of the most important questions in personal finance. It's also one of the most overlooked. The false perception is that this concept is so simple everyone should have it mastered. In truth, while many people can define the words "need" and "want," it's difficult for most people to assess the difference during the most important times: when they're at the mall making impulse buys, or when they set out to create a realistic and effective budget.

What have you heard? That a need is clothing, food, and shelter? And let me guess—that a want is *everything* else? That type of answer goes back to the verbal influences we learned about earlier. (See: *What the heck is a financial blueprint anyway?*)

AFFIRM

I am grateful for all the money I possess today.

Because needs and wants are different for different people, and may even change for the same person at different stages in life, it's impossible to provide a specific and clear-cut list of needs and wants.

I define a "need" as something *absolutely* necessary to your well-being. Does that include clothing, food, and shelter? Yes. But it may also include a cell phone, or Internet connection, or gas for your car, depending on what the necessities are for you to support yourself.

In addition, my definition of a "want" is something you'd prefer to have and which you perceive will make a beneficial impact on your life. Although we can all make great cases for the extras, those wants become detrimental to your financial success when their purchase is impulsive and not planned and saved for within your budget.

Real TALK

A "need" is something absolutely necessary to your well-being. A "want" is something you'd like to have.

When needs and wants go undefined in your financial life, you're left open to continuing to make poor purchasing decisions. If you confuse your needs and your wants, you'll often find yourself temporarily satisfied after a purchase because you bought something you wanted. The problem is you might also often find yourself in positions that don't allow you to take care of your needs adequately or effortlessly.

As a personal finance coach, I often ask my clients to go deeper than questioning their wants and needs. Before every purchase, I advise them to ask these four guiding questions:

Do I need it?
Do I want it?
Am I making an investment?
Am I spending money?

See, when you make an investment in something, you should be able to reasonably expect a return on your investment. When you spend money, you should reasonably expect to get absolutely nothing in return except for maybe a warm tingly feeling and a few compliments from friends. . . And, if you spend the money without hopes of a substantial return at least make sure you're in a position that doesn't leave you feeling guilty because you didn't plan for it, save for it and you know that there were other things you actually needed to invest in to either sustain your life or move it forward.

WHY IS BUDGETING SO FREAKIN' HARD?

Real MONEY

To create a budget you can follow, keep it simple and flexible.

Making a budget is a marvelous first step, but far too often that's where the story ends. Many people give up on using a budget when they find the one they've created is far too rigid, intimidating, complicated, and restrictive. In order to create a budget you can stick to, focus on the following factors.

1. **ATTITUDE.** First and foremost, your attitude toward creating a budget has to be healthy. If you think that budgets stink, then guess what? Your budgeting experience is going to stink! I usually have clients call their budgets something along the lines of a "Prosperity Plan" or "Wealth-Building Map." The title doesn't matter, as long as it gets you excited about managing and mastering your money.

2. **PURPOSE.** A budget should have a defined goal you'd like to achieve within a specified time period. Having a goal in mind will help you keep focused when discipline begins to feel like deprivation. Once utilizing your budget helps you obtain one goal, set another one. Never stop setting specific, achievable goals. Without goals, you'll grow neglectful, and before you know it, you'll let the months slide by without thinking of, or looking at, your budget. Don't become complacent when there's always another goal you can be striving to reach.

Real TALK

Before you can spend more, you need to figure out how to earn more.

3. **SIMPLICITY.** The more complicated you make the budgeting process, the less likely you are to stick with it. You have to think about where you are in life and stick with what speaks to you. If you're relatively young, have no children, and have minimal assets and debts, don't overwhelm yourself with a budget your parents would use. They may have tons of different income sources, assets, and investments that don't apply to you right now. You don't want to have line items there just to take up space on the paper or in your head.

4. **FLEXIBILITY.** The budgeting process is designed to be flexible. You should recognize up front that your budget will change from month to month, and will require at least monthly review. For example, if you go over in one category, then it should be accounted for next month, or you need to make greater efforts to prevent that overage. Remember that if you must increase spending in one area, then some other area must decrease. At no time can you have more outgoing than you have incoming. If you want to spend more, you need to first figure out a way to earn more. Don't get frustrated. It's basic math.

HOW DO I MAKE A BUDGET THE RIGHT WAY?

A personal budget is a finance plan that allocates future personal income toward expenses, savings, and debt repayment. The idea of a budget is actually quite simple, despite the fact that the word's almost a taboo term in a culture that moronically believes you should have what you want, when you want it, and worry about the consequences once you're face to face with financial loss.

To create a budget, you must look at your past spending, as well as future income. There are several methods and tools available for creating, using, and adjusting a personal budget. Although I've listed the most basic categories for you to include in your budget, I honestly don't care what version you use, as long as you use one. Just remember that keeping it simple will keep it achievable. There's no reason for a recent college graduate with no children or real assets to use the exact same budget as a married mother approaching retirement. I've mentioned a few times now that areas such as these should be customized to fit your individual needs and personal style. Keep the parts that work for you, and toss out anything that has nothing to do with your life at whatever stage you're in now. The simpler your budget, the better.

SOME ITEMS TO INCLUDE IN YOUR BUDGET:

<u>Income</u>	<u>Expenses</u>
Earned Income (Money You Worked For)	Charitable Giving
Passive Income	Savings
Spousal/Child Support	Mortgage/Rent
	Utilities
	Cell Phone
	Transportation Costs
	Health Insurance and Medical Expenses
	Childcare
	Groceries
	Dining Out
	Taxes
	Clothing
	Fuel
	Cable (No, it's not a utility!)

See Appendix C for a sample budget.

HOW DO I KNOW IF I'VE CREATED A REALISTIC BUDGET?

On the journey to get your personal finances in order, it's common to hear advice about tracking your spending for thirty days in order to see where your money's going and use those numbers to find the money leaks, cut spending, and create a budget from what's left. Sound familiar? Well, I completely disagree with this method.

Real TALK

The truth about your spending behavior is found in your bank statements.

In my personal experience working with hundreds of people I've noticed something. When people are asked to track their spending, they alter their spending habits. When you know you're being monitored, albeit self-monitored most times, you tend to skew your behavior. You don't want to look or feel bad, so you alter your normal habits and settle for living a pseudo-sacrificial lifestyle to get through those few weeks. Those folks that don't commit 110% will often spend what they want, lie to themselves, and write down what they think looks good. If this is what you're using to set the foundation for your personal finance success, then your entire budgeting process is doomed! It's based on unrealistic numbers that don't depict your true habits and desired lifestyle. It likely includes numbers pulled out of the sky, or numbers based on what you think they should be, as opposed to what they really are.

realistic |rēə'listik| adjective
1. having or showing a sensible and practical idea of what can be achieved or expected.
2. representing familiar things in a way that is accurate or true to life.

A realistic budget is based on a sensible and practical idea of what can be expected in your behavior, not behavior you've subconsciously altered to feel better about yourself. It represents what is true to life. To find the clearest picture about what's accurate in your spending behavior you must look to what you've done already. The past is, in my opinion, the best indicator of future behavior. The past is rooted in your bank statements. It's based on who you really are and what you've already done. It's not skewed by how you wish you looked.

To create a realistic budget, use averages from your last three months of bank statements.

Now that your documents are in order, you can gather your last three months of bank statements and use them to create an average dollar amount of how much you spend in each budget category. These numbers will tell you what areas deserve your attention and where to begin your process of realistic budgeting.

CAN YOU EXPLAIN THE CONCEPT OF LIVING BY PERCENTAGES?

Once you've started on the journey toward a realistic budget for your household, you may logically begin to wonder whether or not the amounts you've set are reasonable. I'm going to go out on a limb and assume you don't want to be back in the same overspending predicament you were in before. To do this properly, you'll want to include budgeting percentages, an important tool most people leave out.

Living by percentages is not difficult to understand, but it's very difficult for many people to implement. This is simply because we like to get what we want, when we want it, and figure out how to pay for it later, as opposed to choosing what we get based upon what we can actually afford.

While there are no exact formulas for figuring out what you should spend in each budget category, many experts in the field have come up with percentage guidelines. They're helpful, but keep in mind that adjustments may be necessary for larger family sizes, ages of children, your area's cost of living, the length of your commute, and other factors specific to your lifestyle. These are simply guidelines that may need to be tweaked to fit your situation. Last year I taught a Mobile Money Makeover for a group of women who I thought would be in their mid-thirties. When I arrived, many of the women were actually well into their early sixties. When this section of the course came up,

they pounced on me. One woman shared that her medical expenses were now a whopping 60% of her income. At the end of the day, you want your spending to add up to 100%.

Here's a list of what I suggest you spend in each category. Personal finance is never a one-size-fits-all journey. Remember to adjust based on where you are in life.

Category	Suggested % of Overall Spending
Savings/Investments	10 – 15%
Charitable Giving	10 – 15%
Housing	25 – 30%
Utilities	5 – 10%
Food	10 – 15%
Transportation	10 – 15%
Healthcare	5 – 10%
Debt Payments	5 – 10%
Entertainment/Recreation	5 – 10%
Miscellaneous	5%

WHAT IF I HAVE INCONSISTENT INCOME?

Budgeting an irregular income is going to be a tad bit trickier, but it's not an impossible task. Although your income may vary greatly, many of your expenses will not. If you have a better than average month, you have to plan ahead and recognize that at some point in the future you could run into a not so great month. You also have to keep in mind that you may not know the exact dates for when your income will come in, and since you don't get to choose when your accidents or emergencies come up, you may very well have a need for extra money before your basic needs are handled.

Real MONEY

Don't include one-time income in your budget. Using misleading numbers makes it impossible to plan properly.

Use the steps below to help with budgeting inconsistent income.

1. **DETERMINE YOUR AVERAGE MONTHLY INCOME.** The more months you can include, the better, but don't use any less than three months to determine your average. If you've had a substantial windfall that's out of the ordinary, or some other income that you know won't reoccur, then don't include it at all. This is your time to create a *realistic* plan for your money. Utilizing any misleading information from the past will only hinder your future planning.

2. **DECREASE NON-NECESSITIES.** Once you figure out your monthly average income, compare it with your monthly expenses. If your expenditures can only be met on your good months, then you have some cutting to do. Your expenses must be based on your average monthly income, *not* the great months that come few and far between. Anything that's putting you over budget, and can be labeled a "want," should be put aside until you can increase your income for at least three consecutive months.

Real MONEY

Until you've increased your income for three consecutive months, delay spending on "wants" that put you over budget.

3. **CREATE A CUSHION.** To plan for unexpected events, I suggest creating a cushion within your budget of about 5 to 10%. In essence, I'm asking that you not budget to the last penny. Every unexpected event that occurs doesn't have to be a state of emergency. What if you're out on a sweltering day and really need a nice cold bottle of water? I'd hate for $0.99 to break the bank.

4. **DETERMINE A DOLLAR AMOUNT FOR YOUR OPPORTUNITY FUND.** No matter how inconsistent your income is, one thing is certain: you must pay yourself before you pay anyone else, if you plan to truly become wealthy. Many leading financial writers may call this an "emergency fund," but I just can't bring myself to use those words. I believe that what you verbalize,

If you plan to become wealthy, you must pay yourself first.

you magnify in your life. So if you wait for a rainy day, then you just might get a hurricane. Instead, create an "opportunity fund" to take care of any possibilities, good or not so good, that may come your way. This will also help you during the months when your earning is below average.

WILL MY CREDITORS REALLY MOVE MY DUE DATES TO FIT MY PERSONAL BUDGET?

Tired of getting your paycheck, paying all of your bills in the next three days, and then waiting another two weeks to get paid again? Not a good feeling, right? If you could stretch a few of these due dates out over the entire month, you could breathe a little. Well, that's just one scenario, but a payment due date can be inconvenient for a number of reasons. And while

If you need to, go online or call your creditor and request a due date change.

you might feel stuck, many companies are willing to work with you. No one is out to cause you a financial hardship each month. These folks just want their money. And the more consistently you can pay them their money on time, the better for all parties involved.

Contrary to popular belief, getting due dates changed is relatively easily. Different creditors have different policies on how to achieve this, but please believe a great percentage do have a policy in place to get it done.

Here are a few steps to follow to get due dates changed.

1. **SEEK HELP IMMEDIATELY.** Don't wait until you've missed a few payments or have been late excessively. On one hand, late payments demonstrate that there's clearly a problem, but on the other, delinquency may weaken your negotiation power. Get help quickly, before you ruin your credit over something that has an easy fix.

2. **CHECK THE COMPANY'S WEBSITE FIRST.** Many credit card and utility companies plainly spell out what's required to change to a new due date. The information is usually found under a customer service related tab, and it will guide you through specific prompts to complete your request properly.

3. **CALL DIRECTLY.** If you can't find anything online, or you're a person that needs to hold a live company representative accountable in case something goes wrong, then find the number to call on your statement or on the creditor's website. You'll almost certainly get an automated message, so listen carefully to the available options and choose appropriately, or you'll waste a lot of time being transferred back and forth. When you get to a live person, specifically request to speak to someone who can assist you in changing your due date. Sometimes you'll be able to request the change over the phone, and other times you'll be told to go online or send the request in writing.

4. **WAIT FOR CONFIRMATION.** Unless you speak to a live person who confirms a new date and tells you when it will take effect, keep to your existing payment schedule. You'll likely have a waiting period before hearing via mail or email if you're approved for the change or not. Confirm the new due date on your next billing statement, and make on-time payments until then, and especially after.

SAVING AND REDUCING DEBT SIMULTANEOUSLY

IF YOU'RE GOING TO make real progress in your personal finances, you have to eliminate the notion that you need to deal with savings and debt in an either/or fashion. No matter where I speak in the country, I'm always asked whether savings comes before or after paying down debt. And my response is always the same: it must be done simultaneously. You've heard me say before that we're either in the habit of creating wealthy habits, (which both of these tasks are, for the record), or in the habit of not creating wealthy habits. Not saving, *or* failing to pay down debt, at any stage in your personal finance journey would put you in the category of not practicing a wealthy habit. Period. Even if you have to start off saving a relatively small amount while you pay down debt, to make the habit a part of your lifestyle, you have to start.

The beauty of getting organized and budgeting realistically is that you should now know exactly what you can put towards either category. Accidents don't make appointments, social security isn't guaranteed, and interest is eating you alive. This isn't a question of whether you can afford to do both. You can't afford *not* to do both. If you need to shift your thinking, do so, and prepare to build savings and reduce debt simultaneously.

WHAT'S THE DIFFERENCE BETWEEN SHORT-TERM AND LONG-TERM SAVINGS?

Whether you're saving for the short-term or long-term, saving regularly is ultimately what's most important. Consistent saving helps you manage your money, plan for future needs, cope with unexpected expenses and

emergencies, avoid borrowing and paying unnecessary interest, and ease financial stress. Still, understanding the difference between long and short-term savings can help you make more informed financial-planning decisions and ultimately make the best choices for you.

You can't afford not to save and pay down debt at the same time.

Long-term savings usually involve objectives like investing, retirement, and children's education. Short-term savings are what you typically hear referred to as your "emergency fund." (I prefer the term "opportunity fund.") This allows you to have money on hand to face life's financial hiccups, both planned and unplanned. Planned events include holidays like Christmas, that vaguely familiar time of year that seems to catch us by surprise. Unplanned events include those moments when you find yourself on the side of the road with a flat tire or discover a busted water heater in your basement. When you don't have savings, these expenses typically end up on a high interest rate credit card, which only makes an already bad situation much worse.

Without savings, unexpected expenses often end up on a credit card with a high interest rate, making a bad situation worse.

Beyond the "emergency fund," short-term savings may also include any large purchases you plan to make in the next one to five years, though funding these goals should come after your emergency money is saved. Major expenditures, like buying a home, planning a renovation or family vacation, expensive dental work, and anything your heart desires for the near future, requires short-term saving.

HOW MUCH DO I ACTUALLY NEED TO HAVE SAVED?

The exact dollar amount you need to have saved can't be determined by arbitrarily pulling a number out of the sky. While there are general rules of thumb, the reality is that your dollar amount will be determined by you, given your particular circumstances and personal goals.

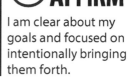

AFFIRM

I am clear about my goals and focused on intentionally bringing them forth.

To figure out how much you need to save in a basic opportunity fund, you'll need to review your budget and look at your income, as well as fixed and variable expenses. You may have heard many personal finance gurus assert that you should have six, nine, or twelve months of your monthly *expenses* socked away, but after going through a time when I had to lean on my savings, I beg to differ.

I believe you should base your fund on multiple months of your *income*. This allows you to pad your expenses a bit, assuming your income exceeds your expenses, which it should. If you're out of work because of an accident, and you've only budgeted to pay your normal bills, how will you cover the increased medical debt, co-pays, and prescription costs that are sure to surface? Not to mention, if you lost your job, should you not be entitled to experience one moment of entertainment? Should you have to literally decide between eating and renting a movie from Redbox? I think you might still want to enjoy life and keep your energy up as you look to attract that next opportunity.

You also need to factor in one to five-year goals beyond your opportunity fund and create a separate account for those short-term goals. (See: *What's the difference between short-term and long-term savings?*) Once you've gotten clear about what you actually want to save for, it's time to research costs and come up with an educated estimate. That amount will be added to your opportunity fund to determine how much cash you need to have saved in total.

Real MONEY

Base the target amount of your opportunity fund on multiple months of income rather than monthly expenses.

In a plainly written formula, it looks like this:

OPPORTUNITY FUND + SHORT-TERM GOALS = TOTAL CASH RESERVE

SERIOUSLY! HOW CAN I POSSIBLY SAVE SIX MONTHS OF INCOME?

I don't know about you, but the first time someone nonchalantly told me to save enough money to cover six months of my expenses, I was instantly intimidated! I remember thinking to myself, "If I can't save $500 consistently, how in the world could I save several thousand?" If that was the key to this whole financial game, then, quite frankly, I felt locked out for life.

Real MONEY

Shift your focus from the larger goal. Saving is much easier when you do it in micro-steps.

Luckily I learned early on that it doesn't have to be that hard. Instead of looking at a lofty goal that seemed so far out of reach, I decided to break my goal down into micro-steps.

If you've been feeling your big saving goals are hopeless, here's what I suggest.

STEP 1: Determine what a great starting dollar amount would be for *you.* (Remember this is not about what everyone else says or thinks, including the experts.) I determined a goal that would seem like a big win for *me!* At the time, if I could get $500 into a savings account and not have a need to touch it for thirty days or more, I was totally winning!

STEP 2: Set your next milestone at $1000. Everyone can think of past personal obstacles that could've been easily overcome, if they'd only had $1000 in savings. *Savings make the difference between a crisis and an inconvenience.* $1000 tucked away can make the difference between getting that flat tire fixed on the spot and having to call-in and tick off your boss again.

STEP 3: Get one month of your net income stacked away. I've had people debate with me over whether this should be expenses or income. (See: *How much do I actually need to have saved?*) I don't know about you, but if some emergency comes up and I have to replace my income for a month, it would totally suck to come up short because I only planned for a specific set of expenses. Heaven forbid you'd like to pay your bills and still treat yourself to a bottle of water on a hot summer day. But maybe I'm asking too much!

Real TALK

Savings make the difference between a crisis and an inconvenience.

STEP 4: Once you've achieved this huge step, pat yourself on the back, and increase your benchmark even further. Keep adding an additional month of net income to your savings goals until you get to at least six months of savings. The target date for each new goal is determined by the amount you can save each month. For example, if you can budget to save $125 each month, you'll have the first $500 in 4 months ($125 x 4 months = $500).

The example below is based on a monthly net income of $2200 with savings of $250 per month. It doesn't include any additional funds set aside for short-term savings.

I will have saved . . .	Amount	Target Date	Date Achieved
Starter Savings	$500	12/01/2013	12/29/2013
Minimum Savings	$1000	03/01/2014	02/20/2014
1 month of income	$2200	08/01/2014	
2 months of income	$4400	05/01/2015	
3 months of income	$6600	02/01/2016	
4 months of income	$8800	11/01/2016	
5 months of income	$11000	07/01/2017	
6 months of income	**$13200**	04/01/2018	

Doesn't this seem a little easier to accomplish than starting out to save $13,000? Imagine if you add in so-called windfalls, like tax refunds. You'll be there faster than you know it.

I'VE HEARD OF AN EMERGENCY FUND, BUT WHAT IS AN OPPORTUNITY FUND?

Several years ago, I wrote an article for the online magazine *Hello Beautiful* in which I called emergency funds dumb. Talk about backlash. Without even reading the article in its entirety, people left extremely mean

comments, and the more zealous readers decided to email me personally and make sure I knew I was a dummy.

Nevertheless, it hasn't stopped me from hitting the road and proclaiming at every church, college, and women's conference that lets me in the door that I don't believe in the term "emergency fund." Most of the finance gurus in America have preached that having an emergency fund is the most basic and fundamental part of having a sound financial plan. Personal finance author and columnist Michelle Singletary suggests that you need at least three to six months of living expenses stashed away for a "rainy day." And frequent *Oprah* guest Suze Orman says, "Emergency cash is a necessity, not a luxury." While I love both of those money mavens and understand the logic behind their thinking, I totally disagree with putting alarming words like "rainy day" and "emergency" in such close proximity to my money.

What's appealing about saving for something bad? What's motivating about creating an account for when you lose your job or your car clunks out? What's stimulating about the thought of a major medical condition overtaking your loved one? It's no wonder more than 70% of America is living paycheck to paycheck. Some financial whiz thought scaring us into saving would work. Unfortunately, it seems to have scared us *away from* saving.

Associating money, something I consider positive, with an emergency, something I consider to be very real, but negative in most instances, just doesn't make sense to me.

What you verbalize, you visualize and therefore run a greater chance of magnifying and magnetizing into your own life.

If you're running around asserting that you need an "emergency fund," what will happen? You'll probably have an emergency! It's inevitable that your transmission will go out, your favorite cousin, who's been dating that loser for ten years, will finally decide to get married and have a destination wedding, and that running toilet you've been ignoring will create a $700 water bill—all in the same month.

So what's my answer?

THE OPPORTUNITY FUND -
AN ALTERNATIVE TO THE EMERGENCY FUND

We should save for opportunities, not for emergencies. Why not focus on the things in life you'd really like to magnify and bring forth? Why not save for a business venture, a dream vacation, a down payment on a home, or some other opportunity that would serve your soul? Why not save for a *sunny* day, the day you actually have the money to take care of something that both matters to you and enriches your life?

Will emergencies still arise? Of course. But now you have the opportunity to turn what would've been a crisis into a simple inconvenience. There's nothing pleasant about an emergency, but knowing you can handle the situation with ease is definitely a blessing.

IF I SAVE ON MY OWN, DO I STILL NEED MY EMPLOYER'S RETIREMENT PLAN?

Your opportunity fund is essentially money you can access in case of an immediate need or opportunity. This is the money you tap into if your transmission goes out tomorrow or you experience job loss for several months. It's not the money you bank on using to get you through your golden years. Your employer's retirement plan, on the other hand, is.

If your employer offers a retirement plan, thank your lucky stars. Many of your peers in the workforce wish they had that option. If your employer also offers a match to your contribution, you definitely want to be in position to contribute at least up to the match. It's free money, so don't leave it on the table.

Here's a look at some of the basic plans you may have access to, depending on your work place.

Real MONEY

Any match your employer makes to your retirement plan contributions is free money. Don't leave it on the table.

401(K) PLAN: This is the plan you hear of most often. It's a corporate, pre-tax, contributory plan, which is payroll deducted, tax-deferred, with a selection of investment options. Most plans also include company matching with a vesting schedule based on years of employment.

403(B) PLAN: Very similar to the 401(k), this plan is a non-profit, pre-tax, contributory plan. It's usually extended to school teachers, church staff, and some other non-profit employees. It may be payroll deducted, and it grows tax-deferred. A variety of investment options are available. Some plans may provide company matching.

457 PLAN: This is a deferred compensation, pre-tax, contributory plan, which is payroll deducted and grows tax-deferred, with a selection of options. Most plans will provide minimal matching.

THRIFT SAVINGS PLAN: This government agency, pre-tax, contributory plan may be payroll deducted, and also grows tax-deferred with a selection of five managed investment options. This plan offers minimal agency matching.

SIMPLE IRA/401(K): Available through smaller companies, this pre-tax, contributory plan is payroll deducted and grows tax-deferred, with a selection of investment options. Normally there is a mandatory match, which boasts considerably lower administrative costs.

If you're self-employed, there are still investment retirement plans available to you.

SIMPLIFIED EMPLOYEE PENSION PLAN (SEPP): This plan allows a self-employed person to contribute pre-tax up to 15% of their net business profit, growing tax-deferred, with a self-directed selection of investment options.

YOU'RE INSANE! HOW COULD IT BE POSSIBLE TO SAVE TOO MUCH OR PAY DOWN TOO MUCH DEBT?

Well, I've been called way worse than insane, so that doesn't sting too much. Believe it or not, between my creation of the "opportunity fund" concept and telling people they're actually saving too much or paying down too much debt, I've been called crazy, and worse.

If you're on my mailing list, you know I frequently host complimentary educational calls on the different personal finance and business topics that matter most to women. I'm proud of the fact that women all over the world who join the calls consider them to be high content and high value.

Right before the recent tax deadline, I held a call entitled *5 Dumb Things Smart People Do with Tax Refunds*, and even though the line was muted, the tweets and Facebook posts afterwards confirmed what I thought might have happened. Women couldn't believe what they were hearing me say. That was the first time someone had broken down the truth about saving for them.

Real MONEY

Yes, it is possible to save too much or pay down too much debt, if there's no room in your budget for those amounts.

There are a few ways you can save too much. First, let's examine what happens when you come into a large sum of money, like a tax refund or an inheritance. If you save all the money, but have credit cards, personal loans, or even a small student loan, then you're technically wasting money by continuing to pay high interest rates while earning little to no interest, depending on how and where you're saving the money.

More commonly, I meet with a woman who decides to start saving without creating or consulting a budget. She arbitrarily chooses to authorize $100 per bi-weekly pay period to go to her savings account. Great start, right? Wrong! If all she can afford based on a realistic budget is $75 per month, she ends up transferring that money right back out of the savings account to cover normal expenses almost as soon as it was transferred in. This isn't great for her savings, but it's even worse for her self-esteem. Initiating that transfer so quickly makes her feel like a failure at finances. She feels as if she can't save, and may even feel that something must be wrong with her. In reality, she *can* save, but she's saving too much for the particular stage she's in. She needs to adjust her expectations.

Paying off too much debt is almost the reverse of the saving example. If you use your refund to pay off debt or attempt to pay too much debt in one month without properly budgeting, but you don't have an opportunity fund in place, you're still not really making progress. Let's say you use an entire tax refund to pay off a credit card balance in April, but in May you have an emergency. Because you have no savings, what are you going to do? That's right, ladies. You're going to put that emergency expense on your credit card. By June, you end up right back in the scenario you were in before the refund came.

Instead, strategically pay down your debt. Definitely put a large chunk towards paying it down, if you can, but leave at least $1000 to the side in an account you can easily access when necessary.

AREN'T THERE FORMS OF GOOD DEBT?

By now, you've probably heard a bunch of bologna about accounts like mortgages and student loans being "good debt." Personally, I don't believe that any debt is good. You may find yourself having to leverage debt in order to make progress in different instances throughout life, but that doesn't make it good. It's still just debt, and your objective should always be to have as little debt as possible. Falsely terming something as "good," makes people too comfortable with thinking that debt is okay somehow. In no instance is it okay. Keep your debt to a minimum, and always have a plan to pay it off. The best debts are the ones you don't owe anymore!

Real TALK

Student loans and mortgages might help you get ahead, but that doesn't make them "good debt."

IS IT OKAY TO BUY STUFF WHILE I'M STILL IN DEBT?

Is this a trick question? No, it's not okay! The quickest way to get out of debt is to *stop* creating new debt. This is the time to sacrifice a little. Buying stuff is likely what got you into this predicament in the first place. You need to use every extra dime you can earn to relieve yourself of the debt you have now. I'm not saying you can't treat yourself every once in a while, but for heaven's sake do *not* go around getting deeper in credit card debt or buying items that are not an investment in your future. This is the time to get mad about the place you're in, so mad that your will to get out of debt supersedes any desire for more stuff.

Real TALK

The quickest way to get out of debt is to stop creating new debt.

If you must buy something, use cash. Credit cards are simply *not* an option. Remember, you and you alone, as misguided as you may have been by others, got yourself into this mess. This is not the time to take the "I work hard and I deserve it" stance. That sense of entitlement will keep you enslaved to debt forever.

WHAT IS A DEBT ELIMINATOR, AND HOW DO I DETERMINE MY DEBT-FREE DATE?

I like to call the debt eliminator system the first cousin of the debt-snow-ball method, which you may be slightly more familiar with. I love using it in the *Mindset + Money Master Class*®, because it gives each participant an opportunity to pinpoint the date they can be debt-free by simply imple-menting a few shifts in thought and behavior.

The debt-snowball method is a debt reduc-tion strategy, whereby if you owe on more than one account, you pay off the accounts starting with the smallest balance first, while paying the minimum on all other debts. Once the smallest debt is paid off, you add that payment money

I enjoy the flexibility financial freedom allows me.

to what you're paying on the next one, working your way up the list, from smallest to largest. The process is continued until all debts are repaid.

The distinct difference in the debt eliminator system is that you use your budget to define the monthly dollar amount you'll allocate to pay down debt.

This isn't about using extra money to make debt payments. How often do most of us even have extra money? This is about creating the space in your budget to uncover the amount you need for your debt pay-off plan. I want you to become intentional and strategic about the money you earn and make the conscious choice to shift from spending without a purpose, to spending for the purpose of paying off your debt in half the time. This puts you in a position of control and empowers you to make wise decisions for your money.

Here are the basic steps in the debt eliminator method.

STEP 1: Complete your realistic budget. You won't know the amount you can actually manage for your debt eliminator unless you budget first. If you start with fake numbers that you can't consistently pay, you'll just feel worse when you fall off after the first few months. The beauty of this system is setting a pay-off date and actively working towards it month by month.

STEP 2: Determine your debt eliminator: the amount you'll apply to debt above monthly payments. How much money in your current budget can be redirected towards the smallest debt?

STEP 3: List all debts in ascending order, from smallest balance to largest. You can also prioritize your debts in the order of the highest interest rate being charged, or by greatest amount owed. My personal preference is to pay off the smallest amount owed first, so you can achieve a win that much faster. The excitement and feeling of accomplishment will keep you on track with the remaining debts. If two debts are very close in amount owed, then the debt with the higher interest rate should be targeted for pay-off first. But again, it's your choice.

STEP 4: Pay the debt eliminator, the minimum payment plus the extra amount, towards that smallest debt until it is paid off. Note that some lenders, like mortgage lenders and car companies, will apply extra amounts towards the next payment. Contact your lenders in advance and tell them that the extra payments are to go directly toward principal reduction. They'll likely tell you the best way to make sure that happens is to indicate your preference with each payment. Credit card companies don't typically need this instruction. The entire payment will go toward whatever the current balance is.

STEP 5: Commit to paying the minimum payment on every debt beyond the one you're actively working on. It won't do you any good to get behind on other payments.

STEP 6: Once an account is paid in full, apply your debt eliminator from that debt to the next account. Both the minimum payment and the extra amount should be added to the minimum payment of the next debt. This new sum becomes your new monthly payment for the second smallest debt.

STEP 7: Repeat until all debts are paid in full.

Do each of these steps on paper first, using the amounts of your new monthly minimum payment to figure out when each debt will be paid in full. For simple numbers, divide the balance owed by the new minimum payment which has the debt eliminator built into it. This will tell you approximately how many months it should take to pay off that debt.

Keep in mind as you go along that you'll be paying the minimum on all other accounts, so adjust the balances of larger accounts by first subtracting however many months of minimum payments will go by, and then calculate how quickly you'll pay off the debt using the debt eliminator. If you do this all the way through, you'll find your approximate debt elimination date.

In the *Mindset + Money Master Class*®, I walk students through this process and provide them with a spreadsheet they can use to plug in their real numbers and determine when they can expect to be debt-free.

WHAT'S YOUR TAKE ON PAYDAY LOANS?

The Consumer Federation of America and the Federal Trade Commission have issued warnings to consumers about the dangers of predatory lenders and the possibility of innocent Americans becoming tangled in debt through the use of payday loans. Instant payday loans are easy to obtain, but getting rid of them isn't so easy. Those companies like to advertise the convenience of their service, but fail to talk about what happens when you don't repay these costly loans on time.

The biggest problem with a payday loan is that a borrower often turns to one as a quick fix to dire financial circumstances. Because she's still in financial trouble when the loan comes due, she can't repay on time. A large percentage of payday loan customers extend the loans far beyond their next pay date. How can you expect to pay off the loan in full when your monthly bills continue to accrue? If you couldn't pay your bills last month, chances are you won't be able to pay those same bills, along with a new debt, this month. This reality usually doesn't hit people until it's too late, and the expensive payday loan debt has made a bad problem much worse.

Another problem with these loans is that they're generally extremely expensive. Lenders are supposed to provide an Annual Percentage Rate (APR) for every loan, but some payday loan companies use the term "finance fee" and do not reveal the true APR. For example, a fee of $20 per $100 for a payday loan may seem as if

UNREAL

When you factor in fees, payday loans often come with an APR of 250 to 650%.

the lender is charging 20% interest, similar to many credit cards. However, the $20 fee per $100 is charged every two weeks. This fee is the equivalent of 26 times that credit card interest! Payday loans can have an APR of anywhere from 250% to 650%.

HOW DO I KNOW IF I SHOULD JUST FILE BANKRUPTCY?

Many people feel ashamed at the thought of having to file bankruptcy. They see it as a failure and an embarrassment, mostly because of the myths surrounding the process and its aftermath. The reality, however, is that not everyone finds themselves in these circumstances due to poor money management. Job loss, divorce, mounting medical bills, and a myriad of other personal setbacks can drive people into excessive debt and create unimaginable outcomes. When these things happen, bankruptcy may be the best option, but you'll have to understand those options and make the choice best for you.

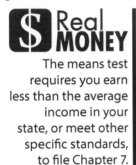

Real MONEY

The means test requires you earn less than the average income in your state, or meet other specific standards, to file Chapter 7.

In simple terms, bankruptcy is the legal process that allows individuals or businesses stuck in a financial crisis to settle their debts under a bankruptcy court's protection.

TWO MOST COMMON TYPES OF BANKRUPTCY:

CHAPTER 7 BANKRUPTCY - Chapter 7 bankruptcy is known as "straight bankruptcy" and is the preferred option for people with little or no property and a lot of unsecured debt. It's a liquidation bankruptcy, meaning the court will sell any non-exempt assets you have to pay your creditors and, regardless of the amount paid off, discharge that debt.

Real TALK

Bankruptcy filing won't discharge alimony, child support, student loans, or state and federal tax debts.

Since October 2005, there's been a means test applied to applicants for Chapter 7 Bankruptcy. You must earn less than the average income of your state. (Check www.usdoj.gov/ust for means testing information). If you're above your state's median, then you can still file for Chapter 7, only if your excess income cannot pay your debts over five years *and* cannot pay 25% of your unsecured debt over that period.

Chapter 7 bankruptcy does not discharge all debts. The filer is still responsible for student loans, as well as previous judgments on alimony and child support. State or federal tax bills must still be paid, as well. If you keep your home or car, all payments on these must be kept up.

CHAPTER 13 BANKRUPTCY - Chapter 13 Bankruptcy, sometimes called the "wage earner's plan" or "reorganization bankruptcy," is quite different from Chapter 7 bankruptcy, which wipes out most of your debts. In a Chapter 13 bankruptcy, you use your income to pay some or all of what you owe to your creditors over time, anywhere from three to five years, depending on the size of your debts and income.

You must have a regular income and owe less than $250,000 in unsecured debt and less than $750,000 in secured debt. These debts must also be non-contingent and liquidated, meaning that they must be for a fixed amount and not subject to any conditions.

Always remember that despite the fresh start you hear about bankruptcy providing, there are definitely long-term implications. Chapter 7 bankruptcies remain on your credit history for ten years after the event, and Chapter 13 bankruptcies will stay on your history for seven years after you file. In addition, either filing will drop your FICO score a minimum of 100 points and an average of 250 points.

I'VE ALREADY FILED BANKRUPTCY. NOW WHAT?

If you've already filed bankruptcy and you're reading this book, I'd say you're on the right track. Besides doing obvious things like creating and sticking to a realistic budget, establishing an opportunity fund, and improving your overall mindset toward money, there are few steps you should consider.

1. **LET GO OF ANY GUILT OR SHAME.** At one time or another, we've all faced financial hardships. Between 2010 and 2011, over 3 million Americans filed personal bankruptcy, and over 6.5 million homes in the U.S. were foreclosed upon. Life happens to all of us. If this has been your experience, there's

Real TALK

Filing bankruptcy isn't the end of he world. Ditch the embarrassment, get educated, and take steps to bounce back.

clearly something meant for you to learn from it. It's time to turn any pain around the subject into purpose. Dwelling on it, definitely won't make things better. Don't be force-fed a host of myths and misconceptions about how horrible and incurable life after financial loss is. Ditch the embarrassment, get educated, and take the proper steps to bounce back.

2. **ENLIST THE HELP OF PROFESSIONALS.** Overcoming financial loss will require time and an intense dedication to financial discipline, but where can you turn for help? The National Foundation for Credit Counseling lists over 700 non-profit agencies nationwide at www.nfcc.org that can help you get back on your feet and set the strong foundation you need during this fragile time.

3. **CREATE SELF-IMPOSED CREDIT LIMITS.** If your bankruptcy included a substantial amount of unsecured debt, then you were likely maxed out on credit cards. In order to avoid ever being in that position again, and to demonstrate how responsible you are now with money, implement a self-imposed credit limit of 30% of whatever the banks may approve you for in the months following your discharge. If you are offered a $600 credit limit, for your purposes the card will never carry a balance of more than $200.

4. **APPLY FOR A SECURED CREDIT CARD.** If you're not instantly offered credit cards, or you're scared to use them, look into secured credit cards. You can deposit a given amount of money, say $500, into a bank account and make it your credit limit. Charge small amounts monthly, pay as agreed, and make sure the card reports to credit bureaus to ensure you're getting credit for this great behavior. Check out sites like www.creditcards.com and www.bankrate.com to identify the cards that work for you.

5. **PAY EVERY CREDIT REPORTING DEBT ON TIME.** After receiving this fresh start, it would be self-destructive to turn around and pay any open accounts late. It actually would come off as if you didn't quite learn your lesson, and while myth would have you believe it'll take ten years to reestablish your credit, you can do it much faster than that. Some filers are

completely restored two years after discharge. If you've a missed a payment or made a late payment within those first twenty-four months, it'll be hard for creditors to trust you going forward.

Financial ruin, such as bankruptcy, is not the end of the world. You can choose to stay where you are, or choose to do something about it. Either way, the choice is yours.

I'VE PRETTY MUCH PAID OFF ALL MY DEBT. NOW WHAT?

Well, if you've banished credit card debt, student loans, car loans and the like, you're probably ready to start investing. There are many theories about when to invest, and some people will say you can still invest while in debt, but if you can't afford to lose a little money without major repercussions, then you probably should stay away from investing. People with little to no debt are usually more capable of weathering the storm you're likely to experience at different points on your investing journey.

AFFIRM

I make money while I sleep.

When most people think about investing, they automatically think about purchasing stock. Stocks aren't bad, but they're not the only investment vehicle you have at your disposal, and they can be extremely dangerous if you invest everything in a single stock. Below is a quick breakdown of a few practical vehicles that are available to you. Make sure to consult a financial advisor to discuss your unique scenario.

STOCKS – Buying single stocks is extremely risky. When you put all of your money in one company, you're risking everything. That can be disastrous at any age!

BONDS – This is the next most commonly known investment vehicle. Bonds are basically a debt that a company owes, and you are the one loaning the company money. Bonds are just as risky as stocks, because if the company goes belly up, so does your entire investment.

Real MONEY

Only invest in real estate if you can do so for the long-term and without going deeply into debt.

ANNUITIES – An annuity is a contract between you and an insurance company that is designed to meet retirement and other long-range goals, under which you make a lump-sum payment or series of payments. In return, the insurer agrees to make periodic payments to you beginning immediately or at some future date. Annuities come in three forms: fixed, variable and indexed, so do your homework when finding the right fit.

MUTUAL FUNDS – A mutual fund is a vehicle through which groups of people will mutually invest in a fund that represents multiple companies. Your risk is lower, because unlike owning stocks or bonds in a single company, if one company in the fund goes down, but several others stay afloat, you won't go flat broke overnight.

REAL ESTATE – Since I was a real estate broker for over a decade, you're probably thinking I'll say real estate is a great investment vehicle. Well, you're right—and wrong! Real estate is great investment, if you can invest for the long term and do it without accruing ridiculous amounts of debt. I've been fortunate enough to make some awesome investment decisions in this area. After college, I purchased a condo in Los Angeles from a probate estate for $160,000. Four years later, I sold it for nearly $300,000. Not bad, right? Well, in the meantime, I also bought a few rental properties in Charlotte and Dallas that were duds. They were duds not because anything was wrong with the houses, but because I was "too busy" to do my own due diligence. For every dollar I made on the condo I lived in, I *lost* $3 to $5 dollars on the other three properties. Moral of the story: Do your homework before you bank on real estate as your number one investment vehicle.

ISN'T BUYING A HOME A GREAT INVESTMENT AND SAVINGS TOOL?

Despite what you've heard, buying a home isn't for everyone. Unfortunately, many people who depended on their house as the ultimate savings tool quickly found out why a home is a place to rest your heads, and not necessarily the best investment ever.

Before the Great Recession, many people who shouldn't have purchased homes in the first place went against their better judgment and bought a house because people said they should. People bought more house than they could afford, and many of them ended up worse off for it. Foreclosure rates skyrocketed, homeowners were forced into short sales, and many of those who held onto their homes found they were underwater on the mortgages.

The old-school home-buying rules (well, not your granny's old school, more like a decade ago old school) told us:

1. to buy as much home as we could afford, or *qualify for*, with as little money down as possible.

2. to buy the biggest McMansion in the neighborhood, so everyone would know we made it.

3. we'd always make money, because homes always appreciate.

Now that we know how awful that advice was, what do we do? Well, it's time to figure out if you happen to be one of the people who probably shouldn't be buying a home right now.

HERE ARE FIVE PERSONALITIES THAT MAY WANT TO WAIT BEFORE THEY BUY.

1. **THE WANDERER. Don't buy a home if you plan to live there for less than five years.** What's the point? 99.999% of your monthly mortgage payment will go towards interest and barely scratch the surface on your principal. Considering the amount of money it takes to make a down payment and then maintain the home, if you only plan on sticking around for a few years, then save yourself, your sanity, and your wallet the trouble and just rent until you think you're ready to settle in one place.

Real MONEY

If more than 20% of your income already goes to debt, don't buy a home. You're not ready yet.

2. **THE NAIVE. Don't buy a home if you don't understand the market in your area.** Who cares what economists say about the national housing market? It's important to understand the city in which you live. Every market is unique. Research the stability of the local job market with a specific focus on your potential industry or those you may be interested in over the long term. Check local foreclosure statistics. No matter how cheap your house was, if folks keep foreclosing at rapid rates, you may still lose money in the long run. Analyze how long homes in your area of interest stay on the market. If homes similar to those you're considering for purchase don't seem to resell well, you may consider changing your criteria.

3. **THE CHRONICALLY INDEBTED. Don't buy a home if more than 20% of your income is going towards DEBT, especially credit card debt.** This is self-explanatory, but let's just say, why make a bad thing worse? If you're having a difficult time paying off $5000, why would $200,000 be any easier? This also includes "good debt" like student loans. (Of course, the only good debt is the debt you've paid off.) Contrary to popular belief, student loans *are* a factor, whether you're building a budget or examining debt ratios in order to purchase a home. If anything, educational loans are the debt to be most concerned with, since not even bankruptcy can erase student loans. Owning a home creates additional responsibilities and financial obligations. If a large portion of your income is already going towards debt, adding a mortgage isn't going to improve your situation, so pay-off as much as possible beforehand.

4. **THE ANTI-SAVER. Don't buy a home if you haven't saved for the down payment.** The days of 100% financing are basically over. You must have something to contribute in order to buy a home these days, ideally 10% to 20% down. The lender needs to know that you have a significant stake in this investment, and won't just bail at the first sign of trouble. Putting some of your own hard earned money into the transaction demonstrates your commitment. Although there are down payment assistance programs you should definitely go after, that should be an additional source of help, not the

Real MONEY

Saving for a down payment demonstrates your commitment to buying a home.

only source of a down payment. If you don't buckle down and strategically budget and manage your money before buying a home, trying to do so afterwards will not necessarily help. And remember, you may need money saved for more than just the down payment. Closing costs, all the fees associated with purchasing the home, are not always covered by the seller in the transaction.

5. **THE UNREALISTIC. Don't buy a home if you don't have a reserve account for repairs and regular maintenance.** The week after your deal closes, a toilet will overflow or a pipe will burst. Things beyond your control will inevitably happen, and you must be prepared tackle them head on. There's no taking the repair cost out of your mortgage like you may have taken it out of your rent. With home ownership, those days are so gone! And beware, because home warranties and homeowners insurance don't cover everything. Stash away at least $1000 above what you save for your down payment, closing costs, and of course, furniture, so that when you do move in, a household inconvenience doesn't become a life catastrophe.

Owning a home isn't for everyone at every time. I'm not saying you'll never buy a house, but make sure when you do, you're actually ready for all that comes along with it. Qualifying for a mortgage doesn't mean you can afford everything it takes to maintain a home.

THE FUNDAMENTALS OF BANKING

TO BANK OR NOT to bank? This is *not* the question! There's no reason for anyone in this day and age to be uncertain about whether or not they should be bothered with checking and savings accounts. If you already know it's not a question at all, but have had your issues with managing accounts successfully, you're in the right place.

Based on financial habits learned from your parents, you very well could be the person who earnestly believes that dealing with the bank is more expensive, less convenient, and less safe than dealing in a world of mattress money and money orders from the corner store. If this is true, I have faith that it's not too late for you. If you grew up thinking that the ATM was somehow a magic box of free money and that your parents receiving those little postcard-size notices from the bank each day was normal, it's not too late for you either. Neither scenario is ideal, but thankfully you have a chance to correct some terribly wrong patterns in your family's financial blueprint. To do so, you need to understand some fundamentals of banking.

WHAT'S WRONG WITH USING CHECK CASHING CENTERS?

According to John Hope Bryant, founder of Operation HOPE, one of the nation's leading financial literacy organizations, "Unbanked individuals are

UN REAL

Check cashing centers charge up to 5% to cash a single check. Cashing a $1000 check costs $50 of your money!

essentially economic slaves," and I couldn't agree with him more. In the technological era we live in today, you're committing financial suicide if you don't enjoy the basic luxury and flexibility of your own checking account. A check cashing service refers to a company that will only do that, cash your check for a hefty fee, and possibly throw in a money order at extra charge.

An argument that I heard while volunteering in an eighth grade classroom for Operation HOPE, was that if you don't make a lot of money, it costs about the same amount to use check cashing services every month as it would to pay bank fees. Another student in support of check cashing centers added that banks were "too far away, and you can walk to the corner store." Look at the financial blueprint already established in such young and impressionable minds.

In reality, banks obviously cash checks, and in many cases at no cost to the consumer, especially one of their own customers. With direct deposit, there's no need to physically cash a check. You can have your funds automatically at your disposal to spend and pay bills via personal checks and ATM or debit cards. With the online nature of most banks, and popularity of electronic payment, it's easy to see check cashing centers aren't really the most convenient option.

As with a bank, you still need to provide identification, and many check cashing services may not even accept personal checks. Worst of all, fees from check cashing services tend to far exceed bank fees. For example, cashing a $1,000 check may come with a 3 to 5% fee, regardless of the origin of the check. That's an average of $40 in fees for a single check! Even a 1.5% fee would be $15. This small loss of income adds up over time, and costs more than any expected benefits of using the pseudo-convenience of a check cashing center. Conversely, many banks that charge a monthly service fee charge about $10 per month.

Opponents of check cashing centers assert that they exploit the consumers they serve, while providing a facade of convenience. Even for those individuals who are unable to open a checking account there are alternatives, such as second chance bank accounts, which provide users the convenience of a checking account without having to pass any type of credit check.

HOW DO I KNOW MY MONEY IS NOT
SAFER WITH ME THAN IN A BANK?

If you have money deposited in a checking or savings account at a financial institution such as a bank or credit union, it's almost always safer than keeping it at home in the cookie jar or under your mattress. The purpose of The Federal Deposit Insurance Corporation (FDIC) is to promote and preserve public confidence in the U.S. financial system. The National Credit Union Administration (NCUA) is the equivalent of the FDIC for all federal and most state-chartered credit unions. You can find current information about these agencies by visiting www.fdic.gov and www.ncua.gov.

Both brick-and-mortar and virtual, or online, banks are protected by the FDIC, which guarantees bank deposits up to $250,000 per depositor, per bank through the year 2013, after which time the limit is expected to return to $100,000 per depositor, per bank. It's important to note that since the start of the FDIC on January 1, 1934, no depositor has lost a single cent of insured funds as a result of a bank failure. The unlikely potential of a bank going out of business is no reason to not open and actively utilize a checking account. If something extreme were to take place, I'm 100% certain you'd be covered.

WHAT'S THE REAL DIFFERENCE BETWEEN
A CREDIT UNION AND A BANK?

I'm a huge fan of credit unions. They're an excellent way to establish a healthy banking regimen because of the flexibility they offer their members. The minimum a new customer of a credit union must deposit is about $5, where banks ordinarily require opening deposits of $50 our $100. On average, a depositor at a credit union will receive a higher rate of interest on deposits than he might at a bank and pay more to borrow money at a bank versus a credit union. No one has money to waste, and when you're just getting things established or reestablished, you shouldn't be in an environment that harshly penalizes you for your mistakes.

There are several distinctions between a credit union and a bank. It's up to you to perform your due diligence and assess which one will work best for you.

Real MONEY

Credit unions often allow deposits as small as $5 to open an account. Banks typically require $50 or $100.

- **CREDIT UNIONS ARE MEMBER-OWNED.** Once you establish an account at a credit union, you become a part owner. That doesn't mean you can walk in a branch and do whatever you want, but it does mean that you receive higher dividends or interest rates on your money, because there are no private investors to be paid first.

- **CREDIT UNIONS ARE NOT-FOR-PROFIT.** This status is why interest rates earned tend to be significantly better, and fees fewer and smaller, at credit unions than at banks. Again, any profits credit unions make are distributed as dividends to their members.

- **CREDIT UNIONS ARE EXEMPT FROM MOST STATE AND FEDERAL TAXES.** This allows them to avoid the need for creative fees that many banks come up with to pass on the cost of taxes to customers. The average penalty for overdrawing an account with a credit union is between $20 and $25, whereas with a bank, fees are usually in excess of $34.

- **CREDIT UNIONS HAVE ELIGIBILITY REQUIREMENTS.** Practically anyone off the street can walk into a local bank branch and open a checking account, assuming they haven't damaged their reputation with a financial institution. Credit unions, on the other hand, require members to have something in common. For instance, your college may have a credit union that only allows students, alumni, faculty, and staff to become members. Virtually everyone in the United States can belong to a credit union because of where they live, where they work, or associations to which they may belong.

- **CREDIT UNIONS ARE ALSO INSURED UP TO $250,000 PER ACCOUNT.** Instead of being insured by the Federal Deposit Insurance Corporation (FDIC), credit unions are insured by the National Credit Unions Administration (NCUA), which is also an independent federal agency that protects the assets of its depositors.

- **CREDIT UNIONS DON'T USUALLY RESTRICT YOU TO USING THEIR ATMS.** Most CUs either offer fee-free access to a huge network of ATMs or reimburse your fees if you use other institutions' machines.

WHAT'S THE DIFFERENCE BETWEEN A CHECKING AND SAVINGS ACCOUNT?

In the early days of banking, a checking account was one that you wrote checks against to pay bills or purchase products. A savings account was an account that earned interest that was paid at varying times depending on the account type. Today, many of the lines between the two types of accounts are blurred, but differences still exist.

One difference between checking and savings account is that savings accounts tend to earn higher interest rates. The higher rate comes from the fact that you're agreeing to allow the bank to use your money to make money for itself. In return, the bank pays you a certain amount of interest on the money at predetermined time intervals. Because of this, there may be more restrictions on taking money from savings accounts than checking accounts. There's usually a limit to how many withdrawals you can make in any given month from your savings account. Be careful. Transfer out of your savings account too often, and your bank can change your account to a fee-based checking account. Read and understand the fine print, or call your institution for clarity.

Checking accounts have both checks and a debit card linked to them in order to provide you with the flexibility to make your purchases or pay your bills. A savings account may come with an ATM card, but you cannot generally use it to make purchases, and frequent use may come with hefty monthly fees attached.

WHAT SHOULD I LOOK FOR IN A CHECKING ACCOUNT?

Although most banks offer several types of checking accounts, free checking has become one of the most popular accounts with any financial institution. Free checking usually means that there are no fees associated with the account, unless you overdraft. However, it's extremely important to make sure you read the fine print. Some financial institutions may require that you have direct deposit, utilize your debit card a minimum number of times per month, or meet some other threshold. There's usually some specific action on your part to keep the account free, or you can find yourself with fees on your "free" checking account.

Real MONEY

When opening a "free" checking account, read the fine print, or you could find yourself paying fees.

Do your research and choose the appropriate checking account based on your individual spending habits and preferred methods of payment. Many people choose a bank based on what's closest to their home or the number of ATMs they've noticed in the area. While this can be right for some people, if you rarely access ATMs or even write checks, then opening an online account may be a better option for you. It all depends on your personal style.

No matter which route you choose, just know that it's absolutely imperative for your financial future that you have at least a basic checking account. Being unbanked is financial suicide in today's modern world, so much so that it has been called economic slavery. Not having a basic checking account closes you off to the fundamental necessities of wealth building. I don't believe I've ever seen a person purchase a home, fund a retirement plan independently, or save for their child's education without having a basic checking account.

Remember, when you research bank accounts, be sure to ask about basic information, such as fees, minimum balance requirements, overdraft protection and guidelines, interest rates (although they are not much on checking accounts), and any other questions you can possibly think of. Don't be timid. Your financial wellness is on the line.

WHAT SHOULD I LOOK FOR IN A SAVINGS ACCOUNT?

Savings accounts are meant to help you save money, hence the name. Therefore, they come with limits, balance requirements, and excessive withdrawal penalties. These restrictions will vary from institution to institution, as well as from banks to credit unions.

The most common savings account is the basic account with a $300 to $500 minimum balance requirement. Anything below this balance will usually trigger a fee, but you can sometimes find special deals with your local banks when they want to increase their deposits. One promotion you might see is a waiver of the balance requirement if you set up automatic transfers from your checking account every month.

Along with balance requirements, many banks impose a limit to the number of withdrawals you can make each month. Generally, savings accounts are limited to six withdrawals per month, with the exception of in-person withdrawals. Any withdrawals over the six will incur a fee from the financial institution and more than likely generate a letter explaining that if you continue to go over your withdrawal limits, the account will be converted into a checking account. Fees will vary, but are usually instituted by the bank or credit union as a deterrent. Some banks may charge a higher penalty than others, so be sure to ask about this when opening the account.

At the end of the day, your goal is to make money on your money, so look for the best interest rates you can find. Generally, you will find better interest rates with online institutions, such as Capital One 360, formerly ING Direct. If you're working to develop your discipline, I suggest online accounts. It takes more effort to withdraw money from these types of accounts, so to turn around and blow it all would really take a conscious effort. Given an average of forty-eight hours for a transfer of funds from these savings accounts to your checking account, you have plenty of time to make sure what you're spending the money on is actually worth it.

WHERE'S THE BEST PLACE TO SAVE MY OPPORTUNITY FUND?

Well, let me first tell you where *not* to save your opportunity fund: in your checking account! Don't give me that confused look. You have some sister-girlfriends out there who have for some reason assumed that they can save within their own checking account and keep a mental tally of what amount isn't supposed to be spent. I don't know who came up with that idea, but if you've been doing that, it's a no-no. It's like trying to diet in the food court at the mall. Just doesn't make sense.

✅AFFIRM

Profitable opportunities always come my way.

Another no-no, in my humble opinion, is keeping your opportunity fund in a savings account linked to the checking account you actively use. Think about your past attempts at saving. How many times did you say you were going to start saving and end up simply transferring money, or even worse, just swiping your debit card, to get whatever it is you wanted, emergency or not? If you're at a phase in this journey where discipline is a real struggle, you probably need to limit access to your opportunity fund as much as possible.

I suggest using virtual banking accounts for your opportunity fund. Yes, the ones with no branches to drive by. The ones with no ATMs lit up during your Friday girls' night out events. The ones that make you wait

about 24 to 48 hours before they'll transfer your money to your checking account. The ones that only start letting you have a debit card attached in recent years, but still allow you to decline to have one, which I highly suggest.

Now, I know what you're thinking. "If I have an emergency, isn't forty-eight hours too long to wait?" Great thinking! Your first $1000 should always be some place you can access with a moment's notice. It still shouldn't be in your checking account, and if you can help it, it shouldn't be in the savings account linked to your checking. It's too freakin' easy to lose focus. You can keep it in cash in a safe place, like a safe deposit box, or in an account for which you don't ever carry the card on your person.

When looking for online bank accounts, do your research. Look for one with competitive interest rates. That's the beauty of these accounts. While they go heavy on the technology, these guys don't have all the overhead of your big banks. That means more money in your purse, ladies. All that money gets passed on to you. Take advantage of it, and get your savings up!

HOW DO I STAY AWAY FROM ATM MACHINES?

The automated teller machine was introduced in the 1960's in an effort to provide bank customers with additional convenience. Unfortunately,

because of the overuse and abuse of many ATM users, banks have used them as a prime means to collect millions of dollars in fees each year. Now there are very few places where you can't find one. They're at daycare centers, inside of restaurants that already accept debit and credit cards, and in grocery stores, casinos, and church lobbies.

You name the place, and there's likely an ATM machine within walking distance. They weren't playing when they said they wanted to make it "convenient."

Although ATMs are more convenient than ever now, their fees are inconveniently higher than ever as well. If you don't have money to save, money to give to charity, or money to pay down debt, where do you find money for the ATM fees?

Here are some tips to keep your ATM fees down, and save the $500 per year that the average frequent ATM user spends on those fees.

1. **IF YOU MUST USE AN ATM, MAKE SURE IT'S A LOCAL BRANCH OF YOUR BANKING INSTITUTION, OR THAT YOU HAVE SOME TYPE OF FREE ACCESS.** Stopping at any ol' ATM because it's "convenient" is yet another lie we tell ourselves. What's convenient about giving money away to huge banks that don't need your charity?

2. **USE YOUR DEBIT CARD AS MUCH AS POSSIBLE.** Not only do you avoid spending more than you need, you have a second form of receipt for all of your purchases. If you lose a paper receipt, your use of cash can't provide you any proof of purchase.

3. **PLAN IN ADVANCE.** Figure out what activities you plan on participating in for the week, set a budget, and get out enough cash at one time to cover at least five days of activities.

4. **LIMIT YOUR VISITS TO THE ATM TO NO MORE THAN FOUR TIMES A MONTH, IF YOU EVEN NEED TO GO THAT OFTEN.** I don't suggest going to the ATM more times in a month than you have pay periods. If your job pays you bi-weekly, than you really shouldn't stop at an ATM more than twice a month.

5. **IF YOU NEED CASH, AND YOU HAVE THE OPPORTUNITY TO GET CASH BACK AT A CHECKOUT COUNTER, GET IT THERE.** That way, you can ask for a specific mix of cash, which will meet your needs and possibly stop you from overspending. Most people withdraw entirely too much money when they're at the ATM. Once they use what they actually need, the rest gets squandered away on unnecessary impulse buys.

HOW DO I AVOID OVERDRAFT FEES?

Ever swiped for a quick bottle of water at the local gas station convenience store and then realized that due to overdraft coverage you spent $36 on water? Sucks, right? That's the thing. Small careless decisions can often amount to humongous consequences.

U.S. banks take in over $38 billion per year in overdraft fees.

While overdraft fees vary, the average charge is about $35. In most cases, this fee is per item that overdraws your account, regardless of the amount. If you have four items that come through after your bank balance has gone negative, four separate fees will be assessed, for a whopping total of $140. Does this sound like a reason to pay attention? Sure it is, especially if all the purchases you made were for small amounts.

You have options to protect you from these fees. First and foremost, it's important that you keep a register or some other means of efficiently tracking your balance in real time. I agree that charging $35 for an item that overdrew your account by $2 is ridiculous, but if you didn't spend more than you had, you wouldn't get the fee in the first place. Take some responsibility, and keep track of your finances. Rest assured that U.S. banks take in over $38 billion in overdraft fees, which equate to more than 75% of the fees they charge on consumer deposits per year. As I often remind my clients, banks are not charities. They'll capitalize off of you as much as *you* allow them to.

HOW TO AVOID OVERDRAFT FEES

1. **KEEP YOUR REGISTER UPDATED.** Simply put, if you don't know how much money is in your checking account right now, then you're at risk of overdrawing your account. Many people falsely believe that keeping a check register in their heads is sufficient. It's inevitable that you'll forget something. Instead, make it a habit to enter each check or debit card purchase as it is made. Set aside time when you get home to check your receipts and balance your register. Do this every time you spend, and soon it will be second nature.

There's no excuse not to know your account balance. You can check it online, by phone, or via smart-phone app.

2. **CHECK YOUR BALANCE FREQUENTLY.** This is a must when you know you're not into writing things down. (No need to deny it. This is about doing what works for *you*.) Take advantage of account information offered over the phone and online. With the ability to check your account information from your mobile phone, there's really no excuse to not be aware of your

balance. Keep in mind, however, that there will be a distinct difference between your available balance and current balance. Pay careful attention to the difference between these two, because the latter reflects the amount in your account minus any pending transactions. Always base your spending on the amount in your ledger in order to avoid confusion and potential fees. If you're just not into writing things down, at least download your banks online banking app, so you can view transactions in real time.

3. **DON'T FORGET ATM WITHDRAWALS.** One of the easiest ways to lose track of your money is to forget to record cash you withdraw from an ATM. It happens to people all the time. They forget to record the withdrawal, and when the bank statement comes, they find out they have hundreds of dollars less than they thought. Nip this potential problem in the bud by always getting an ATM receipt. Place the receipt in a safe place. When you get home refer to the receipt to enter the withdrawal into your register.

4. **REMEMBER TO RECORD AUTOMATIC PAYMENTS.** Having your utility or insurance company automatically take payments out of your checking account can be very convenient. Overdrawing your account because you forgot to record an automatic payment is unquestionably inconvenient.

5. **REVIEW YOUR STATEMENT.** The best way to keep tabs on your checking account is to compare the monthly statement to your check register. Any discrepancies need to be taken care of immediately. If you've done a good job keeping track of your money, there will never be a discrepancy, and that's the goal. You can give yourself a margin for error, because keeping up with the cents can get tricky at times. I like to use plus or minus $2. If I'm under or over $2, I don't sweat it much. But when things are off by $20, I'm on the hunt!

6. **CUSHION YOUR CHECKING ACCOUNT.** Having a little cushion in your account is probably the most effective way to stop overdraft fees when all else fails. To create a cushion, record a withdrawal in your register of $50 or whatever you want the cushion amount to be, but leave the money there. Try to forget about the cushion and carry on as usual. If you

get into trouble and accidentally spend more than your balance, that $50 will be sitting there to take up the slack, and hopefully prevent a hefty fee.

7. **SIGN UP FOR OVERDRAFT PROTECTION.** Usually the protection plan stipulates that money will be taken from your savings first, and then from a line of credit given at a fixed rate. However, overdraft protection generally requires an account with a minimum balance and that the account-holder passes a credit check.

8. **MAKE DEPOSITS EARLY IN THE DAY.** Be aware of the hours in which your deposit will be processed. Usually this is before 4 p.m., Monday through Friday. This guarantees that the money is credited directly into your account that day. If you're transferring online, the cut-offs are usually 5 or 6 p.m., depending upon your bank.

9. **CHOOSE CREDIT.** Run your check card through the credit system, and not through the debit system, by choosing "credit" instead of "debit" when asked. Depending on the merchant, the credit system may take slightly longer to deduct the money from your balance. You'll have a little extra time to make a deposit or transfer funds, if you need to do so.

10. **OPT-OUT ALTOGETHER.** Because of the Credit Card Accountability, Responsibility and Disclosure Act, you now have the option to opt-out of overdrawing your checking account. What this means is that your bank can switch off the feature on your debit card that allows you to go over what you have in your account, and your card will be declined at the time of purchase. The one exception to this is that pending transactions will still overdraw the account. For example, if you use your debit card as credit and sign for it, the purchase clearing your account is dependent on the merchant and when they batch their credit card items. It could take several days to clear the account. If you use your card in the meantime, forget to subtract out the first purchase, and spend more than you have available, that pending charge will clear and overdraw you. This is why tip #1 is to keep your register updated.

CAN I OPEN A NEW BANK ACCOUNT IF I OWE MONEY TO ANOTHER BANK?

Banks are in the business of making as much money off of the accounts you hold with them as possible. It's not in their best interest to close your account, unless you become a liability to their profitability. Your financial institution may close your account down if there's a pattern of writing checks for more than you have available in your account, or if you swiped your debit card for charges that created a negative account balance that you haven't cleared up. If your account has fallen below the minimum balance you agreed to leave in the account for an extended period of time, some banks may also see your actions as a breach of the terms set forth when you opened your account. Additionally, if your account has been negative for an extended period of time (typically sixty to ninety days), the bank's attempts to contact you have gone unanswered, and the issue remains unresolved, they may write your account off as bad debt, close the account, and place the amount owed on your credit report via a third party collection services company.

Failure to maintain a good debit history may result in a number of additional unpleasant consequences. Here are just a few.

1. Your financial institution may charge you daily fees for each overdraft item, making the amount you'll have to pay back far greater than the original incident.

2. The business you wrote the check to could also charge you a fee or refuse to take any more checks from you in the future.

3. You could receive a great deal of collection calls and letters asking you to repay the money.

4. Your name and account information could be reported to a check verification service, which could cause your checks to be declined at point-of-sale purchases far into the future.

5. Your bank could report your closed account to ChexSystems, leading to other institutions refusing to open a checking account for you for years to come.

Real MONEY

Second-chance bank accounts provide an opportunity to get back into mainstream banking.

Don't despair. If you've unfortunately made it to ChexSystems, there's still hope. It's called second-chance banking, a rarely advertised option that many credit unions, regional, and community banks offer to those in your position who are ready to get back into mainstream banking. Second-chance checking accounts are designed to help you develop a better checking record. They usually have a monthly fee of somewhere between $5 and $10 and offer a short list of features like check-writing, a debit card, and online banking. Checks you deposit are usually held several days longer to ensure the funds will clear, and some banks may even refer you to some type of in-house money management course.

Second-chance checking accounts won't include premium features like free checks, debit rewards programs, or overdraft protection, so don't even think about asking for them. Basically, it's never the best checking account that a bank or credit union offers, but if you open a second-chance account and keep a good record, the financial institution usually allows you to upgrade to a more conventional checking account within six to twelve months.

WHY CAN'T I JUST USE PRE-PAID CARDS?

I'm all for using any method that's legal and encourages *young* people to create healthy financial habits, especially when additional options are limited for some reason, or they're testing the waters and don't want to risk using debit and credit cards just yet. But for adults? Nope. I don't agree with it at all. The complexity of your financial circumstances and future goals likely requires that you use traditional bank accounts. If they don't, then maybe I'm dreaming bigger for you than you're dreaming for yourself.

Not many mortgage applications will ask to see a print out of several months of transactions on your pre-paid card. They're looking for good ol' bank statements. Think of what it says to a lender you may want to borrow tens, if not hundreds, of thousands of dollars from, if you can't maintain a basic checking account. Be honest. Would you really trust you?

Think about other long-term goals you may have. Do you believe it seems remotely wealthy to call customer service and figure out how to transfer to your retirement account or your child's college fund from a pre-paid card?

If you've been using pre-paid cards to get you back on your feet, I understand, and I applaud you. But it's time to take this wealth building thing to the next level. It's time join us back in the mainstream.

BOOSTING CREDIT

KINDA HARD TO REALLY work on something and get results when you don't know much about it. All most adults know is that they want "good credit," because bad credit sucks, is extremely expensive, and seriously limits your options in everything from where you can live, to what you can buy, and where you can work these days. Sound about right?

You may literally be starting from scratch and need to build credit. You may have credit that you haven't checked in years, because you're afraid of how low the score might be. Or you may have stellar credit and get more offers for credit lines than you know what to do with. No matter where you may be on your money journey, I've met few people who couldn't use an additional lift.

If you haven't completed Sections 1 and 2 of this book, I should warn you that this chapter won't mean a hill of beans to you. No, really. Nothing I say in the next few pages will have any major impact on you, your credit, or the options I spoke of above. How do I know? Because people always come to me wanting to "fix their credit." Your credit is only a result. It's a consequence of certain actions that originated in specific thoughts and beliefs you've had about different circumstances—those circumstances you created and those you may have fallen into for reasons beyond your control. You can get all the information and education in the world, but if your mindset doesn't change, knowing the ABC's of credit won't change a thing either.

Real TALK

Your credit status, good or bad, is a consequence of your actions, which originated in your thoughts and beliefs.

Well, you've been warned, so without further ado, let's talk about boosting credit.

HOW DO I OBTAIN A COPY OF MY CREDIT REPORT?

In order to keep your credit clean, you have to know what's reflected on it. If you've been avoiding it, it's time to face this thing once and for all. Get in the habit of checking your credit report no less than once a year. Even though you know you pay your bills on time, checking your credit report consistently may alert you of inaccuracies on your credit file, or of signs of potential identity theft.

Real TALK

To improve your credit, you must first improve your mindset.

Request a free copy of your credit report by visiting www.annualcreditreport.com or contacting the Annual Credit Report line at 877-322-8228. Be aware that you'll likely be asked to pay a fee in order to view the full report with the score. The free report is sufficient, if you believe your credit is in good standing, but if you've had any credit challenges or are planning to make a big purchase in the near future, it's important that you choose the version with the score. This will allow you to see where you stand and develop quantifiable goals. You may also obtain your credit report by contacting any of the three major credit agencies directly.

Experian	Equifax	TransUnion
PO Box 949	PO Box 740241	PO Box 1000
Allen, TX 75013	Atlanta, GA 30374	Chester, PA 19022
888-397-3742	800-685-1111	800-888-4213
www.experian.com	www.equifax.com	www.transunion.com

WHAT INFORMATION SHOULD I EXPECT TO SEE ON MY CREDIT REPORT?

Credit reports are sometimes very hard for the untrained eye to review. Study yours until you spot and can fully understand these five main categories of information.

1. **PERSONAL INFORMATION:** Verify your name, current and previous address-es, social security number, telephone number, date of birth, and current and previous employers.

2. **CREDIT HISTORY:** The majority of your credit report is comprised of infor-mation on credit accounts that have been opened in your name. Details about these accounts, including the date the account was opened, the credit limit or amount of the loan, the payment terms, the balance, and a history of your payment records on each account are also included. Closed or inactive accounts, depending on the manner in which they were paid, stay on your report for seven to eleven years from the date of their last activity.

3. **CREDIT SCORE:** This three digit number is issued by each of the major credit bureaus and used to help potential creditors decide how likely it is they'll be repaid in a timely manner. (See: *What's a credit score, and how is it determined?*)

4. **CREDIT INQUIRIES:** Each time a third party, such as a creditor, potential lender, or insurer pulls your credit report, it's recorded on your file as a credit inquiry. Inquiries may remain on your credit report for up to two years.

5. **PUBLIC RECORDS:** Public records obtained from government sources, in-cluding bankruptcies, tax liens, collections, judgments, and records of overdue child support are also recorded on your credit report. Public information stays on your credit report for up to seven years.

WHAT SHOULD I DO IF THERE ARE ITEMS ON MY CREDIT REPORT I DON'T RECOGNIZE?

It's extremely important to look over your credit report with a fine tooth comb as soon as possible. If you discover any mistakes, immediately con-tact all three credit bureaus by either disputing online or by certified mail. No matter how large or small the discrepancy, you need to alert them of the mistake and request that they investigate the matter and subsequently change or remove the item as needed. If you don't get an email or reply in writing within thirty to sixty days, don't just drop it. Send another letter reminding the credit agencies that they are required by law to investigate any incorrect information or provide an updated credit report with the incorrect information corrected or removed.

A sample Dispute Letter is included in Appendix B in order to assist you in drafting your own.

WHAT'S A CREDIT SCORE, AND HOW IS IT DETERMINED?

A credit score, often referred to as a FICO score, is a three-digit number that potential creditors use to help them decide how likely it is they'll get paid back on time. They're also called risk scores, because they help lenders predict the risk that you will not be able to repay the debt as agreed. Scores are generated by using elements from your credit report, as well as other sources, such as your credit application, at the time a lender requests your credit report. Credit scores are fluid numbers that change as the elements in your credit report change. For example, payment updates or a new account may cause scores to fluctuate within a few days.

The designers of credit scoring models review a set of consumers, often over a million individuals. The credit profiles of these consumers are examined to identify common variables. The designers then build statistical models that assign weights to each variable, and these variables are combined to create a credit score. Model builders strive to identify the set of variables from a consumer's past credit history that most effectively predicts future credit behavior.

Your credit rating is calculated by compiling information in the following five categories.

1. Payment history constitutes 35% of the rating. A pattern of late payments will cause a huge drop in your credit rating, especially if you see your score within weeks of the late payment.

2. The duration of your credit history accounts for 15% of your rating. The longer you maintain positive lines of credit, the better. This is why even if I advise clients to stop accruing new credit, I rarely advise them to call the creditor and close the line down completely.

3. New credit counts for 10%, so don't make a habit of applying for credit unnecessarily. This is especially true if you already have outstanding credit accounts that are carrying significant balances. To potential creditors, it appears as if you're attempting to make a lifestyle out of living off credit.

4. The mix of credit used is 10% of your rating. This measures how much of your debt is installment debt versus revolving debt. (See: *What's the difference between installment debt and revolving debt?*)

5. The current amount of total debt counts for 30% of your overall credit rating.

WHAT'S THE DIFFERENCE BETWEEN INSTALLMENT DEBT AND REVOLVING DEBT?

INSTALLMENT DEBT

Installment debts allow you to pay a fixed portion of the total amount borrowed at regular intervals over the life of the loan. The use of installment debt often allows you to purchase items at a competitive interest rate. The loan is paid back using an amortizing schedule or monthly payments of a fixed amount over the entire life of the loan. At first, most of the monthly payment goes to pay your interest. The latter installments go to paying down your principal. The fixed payment amount allows you to easily budget for the monthly payment. It also allows you to have a pay-off date in sight.

Real TALK
Using credit cards to buy things you can't afford is the easiest way to financial ruin.

REVOLVING CREDIT

A revolving line of credit, also called open-ended credit, is made available for your use at any time. Revolving credit usually comes in the form of major credit cards, such as Visa or MasterCard, as well as department store cards. At the time of application, your previous payment history, as well as income, will usually determine your credit limit. Once you use the credit card, you're required to make monthly minimum payments based on the total balance outstanding that month.

Despite how easy it is to obtain this type of credit, or how convenient it may be, this is the easiest way to financial ruin, if you don't use discretion with your credit card purchases. The average interest rate on such cards can be 18% or more, plus annual fees. Impulsive buying, failure to compare the cost of buying with cash versus using a credit card, and purchasing unnecessary items that you simply cannot afford are all part of the demise brought on in pursuit of "convenience."

$ Real MONEY

It can be nearly impossible to pay off credit cards by paying the minimum monthly payment.

A concern with revolving credit is that it's more difficult to prepare for your future monthly payment, as rates and terms may fluctuate based on the very, very fine print in your agreement. It can be nearly impossible to pay off your debt by paying the minimum payment required by creditors, and they know this. Creditors are not lending you money for charity. This is a business, and their sole intent is to make as much money as possible. As you pay down your debt, the minimum payment is also reduced. This does nothing but extend your pay-off period and, consequently, the interest you pay.

WHAT'S THE DIFFERENCE BETWEEN A CREDIT CARD, CHARGE CARD, AND DEBIT CARD?

There are many variations when it comes to those little plastic cards. They all provide a certain amount of convenience, but it's important to understand how different cards work in order to make wise financial decisions. Credit cards, charge cards, and debit cards may look alike, but they offer different services and benefits. Learn the basics of each card, and determine which is best for you.

CREDIT CARD

A credit card is a means of buying goods and services on a line of credit. Credit cards are issued to you based on your income and other information on your credit report and application. When you use a credit card, you're borrowing money against that line of credit, basically money you don't have. You pay it back each month by the due date, and you pay with interest if you haven't paid the balance in full. If you do pay your balance in full before the grace period expires (usually about 25 days), you won't be charged interest. The most common credit cards are Visa and MasterCard. If you carry one of these cards, you can charge goods or services anywhere their logos are displayed or accepted.

AFFINITY CARD – This type of credit card is offered by a bank and another sponsoring organization, like a charity group or other non-profit. The sponsor's name or logo is often placed on the card. The bank typically gives a percentage of your annual fee and purchases to the sponsor. Ever wonder why credit card companies can freely roam college campuses despite the predatory practices they use on students? Now you know why.

CHARGE CARDS

A charge card is similar to a credit card, but it's generally used for purchases during a single billing cycle. Unlike a credit card, a charge card doesn't offer you a revolving line of credit, and you must pay the balance in full each month. The most prominent example of a charge card is American Express.

DEBIT CARDS

A debit card may have a Visa or MasterCard logo, but that doesn't mean it's a credit card. A debit card, also known as a check card, is linked directly to your checking account and accesses your money. Money is withdrawn from your account when you make a purchase, so it's more like a check than a credit card. Debit cards can also allow for instant withdrawal of cash, acting as the ATM card. Some merchants also offer cash back services to customers, which allow you to withdraw cash along with your purchase.

WHAT SHOULD I DO IF I'M TERRIFIED OF CREDIT CARDS?

Honestly, when you realize that a credit card is just a little piece of plastic with your name and the bank's imprint on it, you take away its power. Credit cards are not evil in and of themselves. They can actually be a beneficial financial tool when used properly. It's using them as some type of crutch, or to finance a lifestyle you're in no position to live, that gets you in trouble.

Real **TALK**

Borrowing money you know you can't pay back within the given terms quite frankly makes you a liar.

Borrowing money with no plan for paying it back in less than thirty days is where most people's financial problems begin.

There's a major difference between using credit wisely and having a reckless addiction. Credit cards are a necessary part of how our world functions today. They're great to have when vacationing and for several other short-term uses. The reality is that many potential creditors determine your likelihood of paying them back based on an assessment of your history with other creditors. Consumers who never use credit can be denied a loan or credit when they have a justifiable need or use for it. Using credit establishes a history of financial responsibility. Until you establish or reestablish a healthy credit history, your chances of qualifying for an important loan, such as a mortgage, are greatly reduced. Unfortunately, you need to play the game that the bureaus that score you are playing. You don't have to like it, but you may have to accept the rules and play, even if just for a little while.

Understand that using credit means that you have a confidence in your future ability to repay the debt. Making a commitment when you know there's no realistic way for you to pay it back with the given terms quite frankly makes you a liar. So if you're not in a position to use credit cards as a tool to quickly build or rebuild your credit at this stage, then don't. You've got to be ready and confident that you can overcome whatever issues you've had in the past or the issues you believe you could have based on your unique circumstances.

WHAT ABOUT DEPARTMENT STORE CREDIT CARDS? GOOD OR BAD?

I'm 100% against department store credit cards for several reasons. In addition to the astronomical fees that often come attached to these cards, they're no good to you if you have a minor crisis. You can't use your Victoria's Secret or Macy's card to pay for a tow truck, a doctor's bill, or a locksmith. In the face of an actual emergency, it's just worthless. Having a major credit card provides access to money during the times you may really need it.

Real MONEY
Department store credit cards often come with astronomical fees, and they're useless when you have a real crisis.

Today, more and more major department stores are offering attractive incentives and rewards in the form of cash back and savings discounts to those who regularly patronize their establishments and use their credit cards. Despite how enticing this may seem, I advise sticking to one or two major credit cards to establish your credit.

For those of you that still swear by your Nordstrom's card, here are a few things to consider before your next swipe.

THE ANNUAL PERCENTAGE RATE (APR)

The APR is the yearly cost of using the credit card and may include additional fees or costs above and beyond the interest rate. An important point to remember with many department store credit cards is that rewards, perks, and discounts often come at a price of high interest rates or overwhelming fees. Interest rates on some department store cards may range from 16% to as high as 22%, despite the low-APR pitch you were probably given when you got the card. Those introductory rates may only be good for the first three to six months.

UNREAL

Some retailers require you to charge as much as $1000 before your card starts to accrue rewards points.

READ THE FINE PRINT

Some retailers require that cardholders spend a minimum amount, sometimes as high as $1,000 annually, before you begin to accrue any rewards. By that time you can find yourself riddled in debt attempting to earn a $25 gift card for your birthday. You know that's not smart money management!

REWARDS CARD ALLOCATION

With many department store credit cards, only a percentage of your purchases goes toward earning rewards, not the total amount you spend. And some of these merchants have deals that only apply to customers who carry a set minimum balance on their cards.

THE BIG PICTURE

To earn even a 3% reward on total purchases would require spending $100 to earn just $3. Should you carry a balance to the next month, you may owe anywhere from $16 to $22 on average just because of interest. You've just "rewarded" yourself with additional debt that you could've avoided all together by saving and paying cash.

The key to managing department store credit cards, if you must have them, is to take advantage of the savings, without losing out over the long term by paying extra fees. Never buy something merely to earn rewards, and if you already have a department store card, don't use it to buy more than you can pay off at the end of each month.

CAN I BUILD OR REBUILD CREDIT WITHOUT CREDIT CARDS?

There are several ways you can build credit if you wish to stay clear of credit cards altogether, but keep in mind that the best credit scores are earned by successfully utilizing a mix of different credit types, including revolving and installment accounts. (See: *What's the difference between installment debt and revolving debt?*)

Below are a few tips for building credit without conventional credit cards. Remember that the only way to build credit is to ensure that, no matter what method you choose, the credit line is being reported to the three major credit bureaus. If not, you won't be building credit. You'll just be wasting time and possibly money.

1.   **GET AN INSTALLMENT LOAN.** Applying for a small installment loan from your local credit union or bank may be an ideal way to begin your credit profile. Keep the length of the loan short, no more than twenty-four months, and make sure you're using the money to purchase something worthwhile. Good choices include something that will benefit your business or career, such as a laptop or other necessity. This method should help you build credit, while limiting the amount of interest you pay, and you'll be able to consistently budget for the small monthly payment.

Real MONEY

Be careful with secured cards. Some carry high application and annual fees, which eat away at your deposit.

2.   **APPLY FOR A SECURED CREDIT CARD.** Applying for a secured version of a credit card simply means you make a deposit to the issuing bank or credit union, and you get a card with a credit limit of that amount, similar to a pre-paid card. Be careful with this method, however, because there can be outrageous application

and annual fees, which eat away at the money you deposit. If you bank with one, your credit union would be a good place to look for a secured card. Try to obtain a card that has no application fee and a very low annual fee. You also want one that can convert to a regular, unsecured credit card after twelve to eighteen months of on-time payments.

3. **BECOME AN AUTHORIZED USER.** If someone you trust is getting a loan, you can ask to co-sign with them so that your credit will be linked with theirs. But only do this if you're *confident* the person will pay the loan off diligently. Any irresponsibility on their part will negatively affect your credit score for the life of the loan. (See: *How can co-signing on a loan for someone else affect me?*)

4. **BUILD YOUR OWN PAYMENT HISTORY.** Payment Reporting Builds Credit is an alternative credit bureau that gathers data on rent and recurring payments for cable, cell phone, insurance, utility, and other bills. This may be beneficial when applying for some limited forms of credit, but it's not recognized by all lending institutions.

HOW DO I BEGIN TO CLEAN UP MY CREDIT NOW?

1. **MAKE UP YOUR MIND.** In order to clean up your credit and avoid falling into the same trap again, you'll have to make up your mind now that you want to live a different life and moreover that you deserve to live a life of abundance, not one in bondage to material possessions. Remember, every change starts with a decision. Decide today that if the normal American lives paycheck to paycheck, you're 100% comfortable with being abnormal.

Real TALK

You have to decide you deserve a life of abundance, not a life of bondage to material possessions.

2. **STOP USING CREDIT CARDS.** If you continue to add to the debt, how do you expect to get out of it? When you use cash, it makes you think a lot harder about whether your purchase is really a necessity. Cut up those department store credit cards and put a major credit card in a safe

place for an emergency or opportunity. Do *not* call the credit card companies and close the accounts. That will erase the history as soon as the creditor sends the next update to the credit bureaus, usually within thirty days, and you'll see your score drop. (See: *Why shouldn't I close a credit card once it's paid off?*)

3. **WRITE DOWN ALL OF YOUR DEBT.** List each debt you're responsible for along with its current balance owed, interest rate, and minimum monthly payment. (See: *What is a debt eliminator, and how do I determine my debt-free date?*)

4. **KNOW YOUR DUE DATE.** Late payment fees can cost you an average of $40 per month. This is a complete waste of money Paying on time or early will free that $40 for your savings account.

5. **NEGOTIATE LOWER INTEREST RATES.** Call your creditors and convince them to lower the interest rate by at least 25%. If you've made most payments on time and don't have any negative history, such as returned checks, you'll be surprised at how many credit card companies are willing to work with you. They'd rather do that than take the chance that you'll default and not pay them at all. (See: *What should I say once I get my creditor on the phone?*)

6. **BALANCE TRANSFER WHEN APPROPRIATE.** Transfer high interest credit cards to other cards which may be offering 0% interest for a specified period of time. Make note of when that time will be up, in case you need to shift the balance elsewhere, but be careful to not make this strategy a way of life. The point is to help you get out of debt by utilizing the least amount of money you possibly can.

7. **PAY MORE THAN THE MINIMUM.** As I've explained before, banks are businesses, not charities. Their goal is to make as much money off of you as possible. Credit card minimum payments are calculated to make it easy for you to carry the debt for as long as possible. When you pay more than the minimum, you cut down on the interest and pay the principal down more quickly. (See: *What is a debt eliminator, and how do I determine my debt-free date?*)

HOW DO I KEEP THE CREDIT CARDS I HAVE IN GOOD STANDING?

If you've already begun to cultivate a positive relationship with credit cards, recognizing them as a financial tool and not a crutch, then use the following tips to keep up the good work.

1. **DON'T CHARGE MORE THAN 30% OF THE CARD'S LIMIT.** If your credit limit is $1,000, never carry a balance of more than $300 for longer than 30 days.

2. **DON'T JUGGLE MORE THAN TWO MAJOR CREDIT CARDS AT THIS POINT.** The easiest way to turn this into a negative situation is to overextend your use of credit. With all of your financial objectives to consider, don't complicating things.

3. **DON'T CHARGE MORE THAN YOU CAN PAY OFF IN A MONTH.** Accruing unnecessary interest is not what builds credit. Using the card responsibly does.

4. **IF AN EMERGENCY ARISES, USE A PORTION OF THE CASH YOU'VE SAVED FIRST AND PUT THE REMAINDER ON CREDIT, IF NECESSARY.** I can guarantee you that the interest you'll pay on the credit card is more than you're earning on your savings account.

5. **PAY YOUR BILLS ON TIME.** If you can, set your credit cards up on an automatic bill pay system to be paid on or before the due date. This way, you'll avoid the risk of any additional fees accruing because you missed the due date by even one day. Make sure the date you choose is one when you know the money is guaranteed to be in your account. You don't want to incur a hefty overdraft fee from your bank either.

6. **USE YOUR CARDS REGULARLY TO ENSURE THAT YOUR REPORT IS UPDATED REGULARLY.** This will also keep the lender interested in you as a customer. If you get a credit card and never use it, the issuer could cancel the account. For credit scores to be generated, you have to have had credit for at least six months, with at least one of your accounts updated (or used) in the past six months.

7. **PROTECT YOURSELF FROM CREDIT CARD FRAUD.** Don't ever give your credit card number to someone over the phone or over the Internet, unless you're positive you're dealing with a reputable company or trusted site.

8. **IF YOU BELIEVE YOUR CARD HAS BEEN LOST OR STOLEN, REPORT IT IMMEDIATELY.** You won't be held responsible for charges incurred if it's reported before someone else uses it. The longer you wait, the more likely you are to have difficulties with the process. Policies vary from company to company. If you think your card is lost somewhere you'll eventually find it, have it temporarily suspended.

SHOULD I CLOSE A CREDIT CARD ONCE I PAY IT OFF?

Paying off a credit card is definitely something to celebrate. But closing the account might be the fastest way to cut the party short. Besides having one less card to manage, closing your credit card down might do more harm than good. If you've been working long and hard on your debt, you don't want to get to the end of the road and blow it now.

> **Real MONEY**
>
> Closing a paid-off credit card can damage your credit score. Closing a delinquent account with a balance due will damage it even more.

It may seem logical that paying a credit card off and closing it will make your credit score shoot up, but the reality is, closing a credit card account, even one you've paid off, can actually hurt your score. And if you've heard over the years that closing a credit card that's delinquent will help or magically make it go away, you've heard wrong. Not only is that not the case, closing a delinquent card with an outstanding balance due will further damage your credit.

There are only a few instances when closing your credit card might make good sense. One is when you've experienced identity theft. Closing the account might be the only way to stop the fraudulent behavior, and more than likely your creditor will advise that the account be closed. Another reason would be if it's a relatively new credit card that you don't plan to use. If you already have other open cards, and this one doesn't have a balance, then no harm, no foul. Additionally, if you have a card that for some reason springs new terms on you, like an increased interest rate or annual fee, then you have to do what you have to do. In actuality, the credit card issuer would probably close the credit card for you, if you decided to reject the new terms. Try to negotiate the new terms, or and let the company know you're considering closing the account, before actually doing it.

Here are a few instances when you *shouldn't* close a credit card account.

1. **DON'T CLOSE YOUR OLDEST CREDIT CARD ACCOUNT.** Your credit history makes up 15% of your total credit score. Closing out your old credit cards shortens your overall credit history. The longer your history, the better. It gives potential creditors a clear picture of your long-term habits. Lenders tend to view borrowers with short credit histories as riskier. While closing the oldest credit card may not impact your credit score immediately, years down the road you could experience a sudden and unexpected credit score drop once it's time for that closed account to fall off the report.

2. **DON'T CLOSE ANY CREDIT CARD THAT STILL HAS A BALANCE.** When you close a credit card with a balance, your total available credit and credit limit are reported as $0. If you still have a balance on the card with no credit limit, it looks like you're maxed out. A maxed out credit card, or one that *appears* to be maxed out, will have a highly negative impact on your credit score. Remember that your level of credit card debt, including your credit to debt ratio, is 30% of your credit score.

3. **DON'T CLOSE THE ONLY CREDIT CARD THAT ACTUALLY HAS AVAILABLE CREDIT.** Again, 30% of your credit score assesses how much available credit you possess versus your total credit limit. Closing out this card will decrease total available credit and, therefore, increase your total credit utilization. Basically, whereas it appeared you were managing your credit card well and not maxed out or dependent on it, when you close it, your score is based more on the other accounts you still have. If those still have balances, then you may appear maxed out on all your open accounts.

4. **DON'T CLOSE THE ONLY CREDIT CARD YOU HAVE.** Since 10% of your credit score is based on the different types of credit you have, keeping a credit card in the mix will add points to your score. Leave your only credit card open

to show that you have experience with this type of account. After all, most of the other accounts you'll have are likely installment loans, which are somewhat easier to manage, since the monthly payment stays the same. Dealing with the fluctuations of credit card payments demonstrates a different money management skill.

WHAT SHOULD I SAY ONCE I GET MY CREDITOR ON THE PHONE?

Did you know that the voices on the other end of the phone when you call a creditor belong to normal people like you and me? For the most part, these are awesome people just trying to make a living like the rest of us. They're human, and they've experienced real life, including the ups and downs of the economy, and other triumphs and failures, just like you. So don't let the horror stories you've heard about shady characters, or even your own past experiences, keep you in fear.

Real TALK

Your attitude will determine how successful you are when you negotiate with your creditors by phone.

Your attitude toward the customer service representatives and toward the process has to be in order before you pick up the phone. Remember, your attitude will determine your success with the process. Don't call when you're fearful, angry, or for heaven's sake, with a bad attitude. It won't do you any good, nor will it achieve your desired result. The Golden Rule will truly serve you in speaking to your creditors. Treat them how you'd want to be treated. It'll go a long way in a world where many people who contact them, call with chips on their shoulders.

When you call, have a goal in mind. Be deliberate. Don't call "just to see," or you'll get suckered into results you don't want and probably end up with a bunch of other crap you don't even need. The fact that you're the one calling means that you control the conversation. So set the stage from the onset by announcing, "I'm calling to discuss . . . ."

If you're looking to settle a debt or enter into some type of repayment, use words like "My budget is . . . ." and "I know for a fact I can comfortably afford . . . ." Remember everything comes back to the budget. It's the key to your savings plan and to your debt elimination plan. Don't get talked into something you can't afford and make a bad situation worse. Trust me. The creditor prefers to get you in an agreement you can keep and complete, rather than some astronomical figures you won't be able to stick with after the first month.

Now, no matter how polite and prepared you are, you may get an idiot on the other line. If you do, remember you called, so you're in control. Tell that person, something just came up and you'll call back later. Don't stop trying like many people do. One person's bad attitude shouldn't keep you from achieving your goals.

WHAT SHOULD I DO IF I'M BEING HARASSED BY A CREDITOR?

If you're being harassed, I'm going to assume you've fallen behind on your obligations. If that's the case, to get out of credit card debt, make sure you read *How Do I Begin to Clean Up My Credit Now?* and plan to eliminate that debt.

Now that we have that out of the way, please know, first and foremost, that you're not the first to have fallen behind on your credit card payments, and you certainly won't be the last. One of the reasons banks are willing to take a risk and issue cards to people who may not be able to pay on time, is that they make a fortune on the fees associated with the negligence and naïveté of some borrowers. Nevertheless, you do have rights and you should not be harassed.

According to the Federal Trade Commission's published interpretation of the Fair Debt Collection Practices Act, collectors cannot continuously call you. Section 806(5) prohibits contacting the consumer by telephone "repeatedly or continuously with intent to annoy, abuse, or harass any person at the called number." "Continuously" means making a series of telephone calls, one right after the other. "Repeatedly" means calling with excessive frequency under the circumstances.

If you feel you are being harassed according to the guidelines above, you should try the following.

1. **DO NOT IGNORE THE CREDITOR, ESPECIALLY WHEN YOU KNOW YOU'RE IN THE WRONG.** Acknowledge the breakdown in communication and/or your financial hardship, and make an attempt to resolve the situation. With the number of individuals defaulting on credit cards, smart collectors will be happy to help you create a repayment plan that fits your budget.

2. **KEEP A JOURNAL OF THE DAYS AND TIMES OF CALLS, AS WELL AS THE METHODS OF CONTACT.** You'll need this in order to establish that the creditor's efforts are indeed "continuous" and "repeated."

3. **NOTIFY THE CREDITOR BY PHONE IF YOU FIND THAT THEIR CONTACT IS ACTUALLY ABUSIVE.** Advise them that you know your rights, that you don't wish to be harassed in such a manner, and that you'd prefer your communication by mail. Verify your mailing address with them, and make an arrangement to handle your debt, if you haven't yet done so.

4. **IF THE HARASSMENT CONTINUES, NOTIFY THE CREDITOR BY CERTIFIED MAIL.** A sample letter is included in Appendix B at the back of this book to assist you in drafting your own.

HOW DO I PREVENT IDENTITY THEFT?

Don't be fooled. Just because you haven't been fully exposed to the reality of identity theft, doesn't mean you're exempt. Researchers say that if

Identity thefts result in fraud amounts of up to $54 billion per year.

you haven't experienced identity theft already, you know someone who has. According to the Federal Trade Commission, stolen identity was the number one complaint from 1999 to 2010, and fraud amounts averaged between $48 and $54 billion per year.

With our growing societal dependency on social media and cellphones, we're more exposed to potential identity theft than ever before. In this day and age, what can you do? Many of us use these technological means to stay connected to the world and expand our businesses, so hiding from them isn't quite going to do the trick, no matter how many privacy settings you have on Facebook.

Here are a few things you can do to protect yourself from this costly epidemic.

1. **LOOK AT HOW YOU RECEIVE YOUR MAIL AND IMPORTANT DOCUMENTS.** In many neighborhoods, your mail isn't necessarily secure. You're at the mercy of trusting every person that walks by your mailbox. We like to hope that everyone will be honest, but unfortunately, it doesn't always work

that way. Switch to online or paperless statements from your financial institutions and other service providers, or think about utilizing a P.O. Box. Both are a little more work, but not nearly as much as dealing with the headache of a stolen identity.

2. **MONITOR YOUR FINANCES ROUTINELY.** Far too often, people don't realize their finances have been compromised until it's pretty late in the game, and too much damage has been done. I've found that for many people getting the mail out of the mailbox is one thing, but actually opening it up and reading it is another. You need to know what's going on with anything associated with your name and social security number. Don't ignore envelopes from companies you didn't open an account with. If they're sending you correspondence, maybe somebody else opened an account in your name.

3. **CHECK YOUR CREDIT OFTEN.** By "often," I mean more than that one time of year you can get the free report from annualcreditreport.com. You can find credit monitoring services through your financial institution or the credit bureaus. You want to receive an alert as soon as a new account is applied for or opened in your name.

4. **USE MORE THAN ONE PASSWORD.** I know, I know. It seems like too much trouble to memorize all these passwords, but if it keeps a crook off your heels and out of your wallet, isn't it worth it? Use PINs and passwords with numbers, symbols, and upper and lowercase letters that are difficult to guess. Remember, difficult means difficult. If I know your spouse's name and children's names ten minutes after meeting you and can use that information to crack your passcodes, you probably need to put a little more creativity into it.

5. **TRY OUT AN IDENTITY PROTECTION SERVICE.** Think about this like car insurance. You can have a black belt in defensive driving, but the reality is you're still at the mercy of other drivers. If someone hits you, isn't it great to be able to call your insurance company and have them handle all of the paperwork, phone calls, and negotiations? If your identity is stolen, identity protection services can do the exact same thing.

Did you know that the average victim spends 165 hours working to close accounts opened in their name due to ID theft? They spend another fifty-eight hours correcting problems on existing accounts. Unless you can take three full weeks off of work to make this your full-time job, you may want to consider identity protection. Look specifically for services like Protect My ID, offered by the credit bureau Experian. Not only do they assign a person to handle your case and cut down the time you'd otherwise spend getting your life back together, they offer credit monitoring to ensure it'll never happen again.

Every day, somewhere in this country, an identity theft victim loses the opportunity to realize his or her dreams. Whether it's the opportunity to obtain financing for a mortgage or an auto loan, or to take out a student loan to complete a degree, dreams are crushed because of lack of planning and preparation in this area. Get serious about making sure it doesn't happen to you.

RELATIONSHIPS AND MONEY

RELATIONSHIPS MATTER. FOR THE most part, we do what we do, live where we live, drive what we drive, work where we work, and are who we are because of the relationships we've experienced in our lives.

From the financial blueprints we inherited from those who had influence over us as young people, to those romantic relationships we've chosen to allow into our lives, to the influence we have over our own children—we are constantly in relationship. And no matter how well you create wealthy habits, how much more money you earn, or how well you manage your money, you can still find yourself in a financial pickle if you don't learn to manage the conversations you have about money with the ones you love.

A money-etiquette survey from 2007 found that "57% of people said they have seen a friendship or relationship ruined because one person didn't pay back the other." If you've ever experienced the guilty pleasure of a daytime court TV show, you've witnessed children suing their parents, neighbors and best friends battling over broken promises, and brothers and sisters taking sibling rivalry to a whole new level, with money at the center of it all.

Because we're all constantly in relationship with others, at some point we'll likely face one of these awkward and potentially hurtful scenarios. Does that mean you should avoid these money conversations like the plague? Does that mean you don't discuss differences, because you don't want to argue? Does that mean you don't tell people *no*, because you don't

A survey found that 57% of people have seen a relationship ruined due to one party's failure to repay the other.

want anyone to be mad at you? Absolutely not. It means you must learn to communicate effectively about the subject of money.

You can't have a great relationship with anyone on any level until you learn how to have these discussions. Is it always an easy task? Not at all. But if you don't learn to manage conflicts and have civilized conversations about money, you risk losing family members and good friends. That won't be easy to accept either. You can be reactive or proactive, but the topic of relationships and money will come up over and over again. How you handle it is up to you.

YOUR HONEY, YOUR MONEY

L ET'S TEST YOUR KNOWLEDGE quickly. What's the number one cause of divorce in America today? Drum roll please. . . .

NOT money!

On a 2012 list of Top 10 reasons couples divorce, money finally slipped down to number four. But guess what rose to the top. Communication breakdown. For many people, the issue happens to be communicating about money.

Where does all this poor communication start? Think about your dating relationships, past or present. Money is the one subject folks will lie about most when they're testing the dating waters with someone new. People tend to stretch the truth a bit when it comes down to talking about the dollar. They do all kinds of things to influence how others perceive their finances. While some conceal their money to be certain they're not being used for it, others spend money they don't have in an attempt to impress the objects of their affection. Some people hide behind a facade of the disciplined fiscal manager to cover up the fact that their finances are in complete shambles. This may work in surface level interaction, ladies, but when dating becomes a full blown relationship, it's time to get real.

When disagreements arise around "little" financial issues, they often lead to much bigger challenges. From shared financial responsibilities to unequal earning, we don't want these issues to snowball into the other top causes of divorce: infidelity and physical, psychological, or emotional abuse. It's time to talk money with your honey!

WHAT ARE THE WARNING SIGNS OF A FINANCIALLY IRRESPONSIBLE PERSON?

He's clean-cut, drives a luxury sedan, and lives in a nice neighborhood, huh? On the surface, a lot of guys come across as having it all together. Could anyone look at you and tell you've been involved in some risky financial behavior? Didn't think so.

Real TALK

Before dating becomes "I do," look for warning signs of risky financial behavior. If you find them, act accordingly.

No matter how financially successful a person looks on the outside, it's up to you to be alert and pay attention to the waving red flags that make it clear this stud might really be a bit of a dud with his money. Each year, many couples split over financial disagreements, but please be clear. People who end a marriage over bad money habits didn't develop those habits after they married. They had them all along, and the signs were there. Before dating becomes "I do," look for these warning signs and clues. If you find them, run or sign up for some serious premarital counseling before walking down the aisle.

RED FLAG #1: He drives a big flashy car and lives in a fly apartment, the one he calls a "condo," in the ritzy part of town, while his furniture consists of a futon and a sixty-inch flat screen television. Okay, if he moved in last Saturday, then you can give him a pass, but if he's a grown man and has been there longer than a year with no real furniture, chances are he's not the baller you thought he was. I don't care how much he travels for work. The only thing worse would be him living in a fully furnished home—with his mama!

RED FLAG #2: When you met him, he was buying out the bar at the club or picking up the tab at happy hour. But every time you visit that empty apartment, his refrigerator's also empty, with the exception of the Arm & Hammer Baking Soda he uses to keep the ice fresh. Be leery of anyone who's so concerned with impressing complete strangers on Saturday night, he'll starve for the rest of the week. Not a financially savvy trait.

RED FLAG #3: Have you ever seen him get his mail out of the mailbox? If not, be concerned. He can't have control of his finances if he's ignoring his mail.

A man who has his finances together won't run the risk of missing something important. On the flip side, if he does get the mail, but the contents are always pastel colored envelopes that read "URGENT" or "PAST DUE" across the front, you should really be concerned. That's a pretty standard clue that he's having trouble paying his bills on time.

RED FLAG #4: He never answers his phone when you're around. Initially, you may assume it's another woman, but once you catch a glimpse of the phone flashing once or twice, you realize he's ignoring 800 numbers, and we're all experienced enough to know that's the universal sign of a creditor that means business. More than likely he owes some big money. Paying the light bill a few days late doesn't typically warrant those aggressive collection calls.

RED FLAG #5: He doesn't have a bank account. You thought buying everything with cash was a part of his "all cash" money management system. Now you realize he has no checking account, ATM card, or debit card. If he explains this with anything remotely close to, "Check cashing places are cheaper," politely excuse yourself and run for cover. With that type of thinking, he'll be putting his debt in your name in no time.

I know these examples are somewhat humorous, but if you have your finances on the right track, or are making strides to get them there, you must be careful of the company you keep, especially those you choose to date. Although you may have the best of intentions to help him get his finances straight, it's much easier for him to screw yours up. Don't ignore the signs. They're all around you, if you just pay attention.

ARE THERE QUESTIONS I SHOULD ASK ABOUT MONEY WHILE WE'RE DATING?

While you're definitely on point in your desire to have an upfront money conversation with the man in your life, don't get the questions completely out of order. When we first start dating someone, we all too often jump straight into asking how much money they make. If we like what we hear, we stick around. But you

Real TALK

"How much do you make?" is definitely not the first money question you should ask when you're dating.

already know by now that whether your guy is making $40,000 per year or $400,000 per year, if he doesn't manage it well, or you two lack financial compatibility, you'll still have issues.

Here are a few appropriate questions to get your financial discussions rolling.

1. *How did your parents handle money?*

We all have a financial blueprint, the way we specifically interact with our money. For most of us, this was handed down to us by our parents almost like a strand of DNA. But it's important to remember no one is born with a particular attitude towards money. We were all taught specific ways to think about and deal with money matters. These conscious and subconscious beliefs, ideals, thoughts, and actions are what create our financial blueprint.

Talk to each other about what you've heard about money and what types of behaviors you've witnessed regarding money and financial matters. Once you can understand the environment a person grew up in, or the way his parents or other influential people in his life handled money, it'll be much easier and much less frustrating to understand his money style.

2. *What does money really mean to you?*

When it comes to our relationships, money is *not* the issue many people believe it is. Money, that little green piece of paper in your wallet, in and of itself, is powerless. It's actually what the money represents to two different individuals that can be problematic.

Money represents different things to different people. Money and material items might equate to love and affection for some. For others, they could represent the difference between dependency and control or between safety and instability. If a person grew up in a family that exchanged expensive presents as signs of love and affection, they might expect to get the same treatment from a partner in adulthood. But suppose that partner was raised to believe working hard, saving money, and providing a stable home environment meant love and affection? These two people, both of whom mean well, are likely to bump heads.

3. *Despite our differences, how can we create and commit to shared financial goals?*

Here's where having a "So what, Now what?" attitude comes in handy. If you're not going to break up over the fact that you're a spender and he's a saver, then it's time to figure out what goals are most important to you, individually and as a couple. If it's too early in the relationship to be considering larger goals together, then create individual goals and hold each other accountable. Now that you know each other's financial strengths and weaknesses, don't use them as tools to condemn one another. Use them to empower each other to be better, do better, and achieve more.

Use each other's financial strengths and weaknesses to empower each other.

I PREFER TO DATE MEN WITH MONEY. DOES THAT MAKE ME A GOLD DIGGER?

Many women want to take the spontaneous approach to falling in love. Boy meets girl. It's love at first sight, and they live happily ever after. Others have a more practical approach, which for some reason seems to be both admired and despised in our culture.

While we condemn people who appear to marry for monetary gain instead of love, we flock to mainstream media shows about the wives, girlfriends, or mistresses of wealthy men. We glorify their luxurious lifestyles, even though we know that a majority of these women are terribly broken inside.

A man is not a financial plan.

The dictionary defines a gold digger as a "person who dates others purely to extract money from them, in particular a woman who strives to marry a wealthy man."

If the stiletto fits, then wear it proudly. On the other hand, if you don't date men "purely" to extract money from them, then take the insinuations of others with a grain of salt. Still, I can't let you go without reminding you I don't believe a man should be *any* woman's financial plan.

Reality television may be feeding young women delusions of grand lifestyles, but I can't place all the blame on the media. Yes, these shows tell young women the only control they have over their financial destinies is staying fly enough to trap, I mean, to *catch* a baller. Yes, I regularly criticize 50 Cent for the hook, "Have a baby by me and be a millionaire," when I speak to high school and college girls across the country. But here's the truth. Long before rap artists and cable television, many women were taught that—no matter how educated they were—their primary job was to find a suitable man to provide for them. Although times have changed, similar advice still runs rampant.

Years ago, after I spoke at a university in Georgia, a college freshman e-mailed me to say that although she understood my point, she still faced a mother and grandmother who told her daily that a man would be her golden ticket to a good life and financial independence. I feel safe in saying her granny didn't get that idea from the *Real Housewives* of anywhere. Instead of lawyers and doctors, many young women today are being encouraged to scout athletes and entertainers to find the lucky guy who gets to be their retirement plan, assuming he doesn't "MC Hammer" his fortunes away.

To these young ladies I continue to offer the bumper sticker mantra, "A man is not your financial plan," and here are three reasons why.

1. **YOUR MAN WON'T ALWAYS BE AROUND.** We all know divorce rates are high, but can we get some stats on the break-up rates for non-married couples? In my business, I coach women who've been left with thousands of dollars in debt by boyfriends. Yes, you read correctly, B-O-Y-F-R-I-E-N-D-S! And no matter, how mad folks get at me, I stand firm in my belief that women must stop treating boyfriends like husbands. Rushing into that kind of behavior is one surefire way to financial ruin.

Real TALK

Women need to stop treating boyfriends like husbands. Rushing into that behavior is a sure path to financial ruin.

From car notes to apartment leases they couldn't afford, I've seen women who signed their names on the dotted line because a man told them he'd be responsible for the payments. Oldest trick in the book, ladies. Did we learn nothing from actress Lisa Raye? Her former husband, the Prime Minister of Turks and Caicos, supposedly worth $180 million at the time, "gave" her a Rolls Royce Phantom as a gift while they were dating. Somehow though, it had a $6500 note on it, which ended up in her name. Now just how does that happen?

Even if you're in a stellar relationship with the man of your dreams, at some point your relationship will end, if only because life ends. Statistics continue to show that women live several years longer than men. If that's the case for you down the road, think about what could happen if your husband is the only one who knows anything about the family finances. At a time when widows should be left to mourn, many are left scurrying to locate insurance policies that may not even exist. Nothing's worse than believing everything's taken care of financially and finding out quite the opposite is true after it's too late.

2. **YOUR MAN MAY NOT BE GOOD WITH MONEY.** It's typical for me to meet a woman who declares she's waiting to get married so her future husband can take control of her finances. Let's make sure that you bring something to the table. And by that, I don't just mean contributing your own money, but also your own healthy money mindset. Why should some poor unsuspecting soul inherit your bad credit, bad habits, and bad financial package? You may be fine, but not that fine!

You should come to a relationship with your finances in order *and* your knowledge pulled together, in case you don't get blessed with a guy who's good with money. What if your Prince Charming is worse with personal finance than you are? Do you turn down his proposal, or do you strap on your high heels and get down to business? The days of men automatically taking responsibility for handling the family finances are over. It's time to assign one of your family's most important tasks to whoever is better suited to manage it efficiently. Remember when the money is funny, so is your honey. Get involved, and be aware at all times of what your assets, debts, and household expenses are, no matter who handles the money on a daily basis.

3. **PERSONAL FINANCE IS ABOUT PERSONAL RESPONSIBILITY.** Bottom line: your personal finances are solely your responsibility. If you're grown, it's not your parent's obligation anymore, nor is it the responsibility of the partner you choose, to take care of your finances. At each stage in life, you must take ownership of your own money. The minute you depend on anyone else to handle your finances, you hand over the control of your financial destiny, and your life goes wherever *they* want to take it. When you aren't in control of your money, you're forever at the mercy

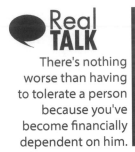

of others, forced to ask, "How high?" every time they say, "Jump."

You must be ready, willing, and able to manage your finances at all times, with or without a man in the picture. When you are, you have the power, and you are in control. You call the shots, and you have the ability to make the decisions you believe will benefit you the most. There's nothing worse than having to tolerate a person because you've allowed yourself to become financially dependent on him.

A man is a partner, a companion, someone to share your life with. He's not your financial plan. And if after reading all this you realize the gold-digging stiletto fits, don't be mad if someone calls you out on it.

WHAT SHOULD I DO IF DISCOVER MY MATE IS FUNDAMENTALLY BAD WITH MONEY?

Well, first of all, don't make yourself sound like a saint or a victim, because more than likely he didn't become irresponsible this far into the relationship. You're dealing with the residuals of not having open and honest conversations about money habits and financial blueprints in the beginning. Early conversations aside, are you 100% positive you didn't notice any of the signs before things got serious? . . . I'll wait.

I'm not blaming you. I'm encouraging you to take ownership of your part in the situation. Your mate probably showed you his true colors long before diamond rings, a shared home, and cute little babies entered into the picture. (See: *What are the warning signs of a financially irresponsible person?*) As they say, when people show you who they really are, believe them. Accept that you'll never be able to change anyone but yourself.

Okay, okay. Enough crying over spilled milk. Now that you're at this place, don't become a nag about it. Do whatever it takes to set the right mood to have an honest, judgment-free conversation with your honey. (See: *Are there questions I should ask about money while we're dating?*) No matter how difficult the talk is to have, you can't create a truly great relationship until you can openly communicate about this topic. Trust me, once you can talk about money without getting defensive or blowing up, you'll be able to talk about anything.

HOW CAN I MAKE MY MAN BETTER WITH MONEY?

Let's be clear. You really can't *make* anyone but yourself better with money. You can motivate your significant other and encourage him as much as possible, but if you think you can just change him, girlfriend, you better think again!

Remember, everyone has their own financial blueprint, and had you taken time to ask the right questions while you were dating, you would know his by now. No worries though.

Real TALK

If you think you can change your man, think again!

Even though he's already officially your man, it's not too late. Use the steps below to help your man with his money.

1. **GET BACK TO THE BASICS.** If neither of you knows why your man interacts with money the way he does, neither of you will be able to help him make progress. Start with the basic questions all couples should know about one another. (See: *Are there questions I should ask about money while we're dating?*)

2. **CREATE A SAFE SPACE.** Once you know what his money personality is, don't become judgmental. It's not your job to be his financial fairy godmother, lurking over every purchase or financial decision he makes. Become a resource for him. If he opens up enough to ask you for help, give it freely. Leave all of your smart comments, irritable sighs, and looks of disgust at the door, no matter how frustrated you are. You promised to help, so be helpful.

3. **WORK AS A TEAM.** If your man is actually willing to acknowledge his money skills could use some fine-tuning, don't leave him on his own. Work with him. Offer to help him set up a budget, open the proper bank accounts, hire the right financial professionals, or whatever else he needs. Don't nag him to death. Be supportive, and change your mindset from what *he* needs to get done to what *we* need to get done.

4. **LEAD BY EXAMPLE.** When all else fails, keep doing you, if what you're doing is right. If you're notorious for imposing rules you don't follow, then you can forget about him jumping on the bandwagon anytime soon. Be the change you would like to see in him. Eventually he may come around. If he doesn't, you have some tough choices to make.

I MAKE MORE MONEY THAN MY MAN. WHY DO I FEEL LIKE HE CAN'T HANDLE THAT?

According to a 2012 *USA Today* analysis of the U.S. Census Bureau, you're not alone if you're making more money than your man. In a record 23% of families, women are the primary breadwinners, out-earning their husbands by 28% when both spouses work. This means the wife is bringing home the bacon, or at least more bacon than her husband, in more than 12 million American families.

Now that you know you're not alone, are you absolutely sure your man can't handle it? Give these questions some thought.

1. **ARE *YOU* SELF-CONSCIOUS ABOUT YOUR MAN EARNING LESS?** Among the women I've coached in this position, I've noticed a consistent general assumption: because she earns more, the man must be upset or self-conscious. In reality, I've found many of the women were actually the self-conscious half of the relationships and projected those feelings on to their mates.

    I know several women in entertainment and other professions who make quite a bit more than their men. When we're out and about, you'd never know the difference. Not only do the women make it a non-issue, the men seem to wear their confidence quite well.

2. **ARE YOU HANDLING YOUR SUCCESS GRACEFULLY?** No matter how fine you are, arrogance is not attractive. If you're the type of person that enjoys reminding everyone who you are, what you've accomplished, and what you buy for whom, you're probably going to have a difficult time in any relationship. The first thing to understand is that your money and position are *not* your identity. A job title is just a job title. That's not you. And neither is your degree, money, or professional standing. Put the

shoe on the other foot. If a man constantly reminded you of who he was and what he had, would you really want to put up with him?

EACH TIME MY MATE AND I DISCUSS MONEY, THINGS GET TENSE. HOW CAN WE GET THROUGH THIS?

For the first few years of my marriage, things were tight. We'd been business partners in the real estate firm, each of us earning well into six figures, since college. By the time we got married, the real estate market was tanking, and we were living off savings. We went from eating out for breakfast, lunch, and dinner to lingering around the house until one of us couldn't take the hunger anymore and broke down and cooked. It was tough.

Real TALK

When it comes to money, compromise can leave you both feeling like losers.

Not only were we dealing with merging our finances, we were each struggling with the fact that we didn't have many finances to manage anymore. It took quite a few sessions of counseling, and periods of going at each other's throats, before we realized we were stressed and taking it out on one another. As the pastor administering our couple's counseling reminded us, "When your money becomes funny, so does your honey."

My husband and I have learned:

1. **TIMING IS EVERYTHING.** Early on in our marriage, I wanted to discuss issues when it was convenient for me, which happened to be the moment they came up. The idea of waiting until a better time presented itself, or until I was in a calmer mood, didn't even cross my mind. If I wanted to call my husband in the middle of the day about a bill, I would. If I wanted to wake him up in the middle of the night, I would. If I wanted to get something off my chest as soon as he walked through the door, you guessed it. I would. And if he wasn't in the mood to deal with my shenanigans, I felt like he didn't care about our bills, or our credit, or getting out of debt as much as I did. Wrong.

   My husband eventually taught me how to bring things to his attention, and I was willing to learn for the sake of our relationship. Now I know that when he gets home from work, I've got to give him a little time to unwind from the day. Waiting also gives me time to process the situation, so I'm not as emotional. I can present the facts, and we can solve any issues logically and as a team.

2. **COMPROMISE ISN'T BENEFICIAL.** I know it goes against much of what you've probably learned, but when it comes to money, compromise can leave you both feeling like losers. With this sort of lose-lose solution, neither person gets what they want, and one or both of you ends up feeling cheated. A win-win solution, by contrast, occurs when your way meets his way and creates our way. Get clear about the specific underlying concerns you're both having, and address those. Work together and come up with specific solutions to address each smaller concern that's creating big blowouts over money.

3. **DON'T PLAY THE BLAME GAME.** After you have a huge disagreement about money, you might be tempted to try and figure out who's at fault. Remember you both learned how to interact with money in different ways. Neither of you is wrong, per se, just different. If you use words like, "you should have," or "you're the reason why," you're not actually trying to resolve the issue. You're aggravating the situation by making the other person feel defensive.

   Instead of blaming your partner for what's not working, look back at your own behavior and ask yourself what you can do differently in the future. It's not your job or your right to decide what your partner should do differently. Focus on your own behavior. Start telling your partner, "Next time I think I could," and see how that changes the tone of the conversation.

HOW DO WE DECIDE WHO SHOULD MANAGE THE MONEY?

If you're asking this question, you've clearly dismissed the archaic belief that men should automatically manage the household finances simply because they're men. When I got heavily into real estate in my early twenties, most of the clients I served were older than I was by ten, twenty, or even thirty years. I can't tell you how many stories I heard from women who suffered financial abuse at the hands of men they trusted with their financial lives. Whether it was the widow or divorcee who assumed everything was set up to protect her in case of any crisis, or the married woman who only discovered once it was time to buy a house that her family didn't have nearly the money saved that she was led to believe, it taught me a valuable lesson about shared financial responsibility and staying involved.

As many married folks will tell you, and behavioral economists confirm, a major benefit of marriage is that it lets you focus on what you're good at, whereas your spouse can contribute from his strengths. While my husband might be good at earning money, I'm good at running the household. This is something we hashed out way back in premarital counseling. The key is that we don't keep each other in the dark. If anything ever happens to one of us, we each know how much we spend monthly, the location of savings and investments, and how to access the funds. We sit down and discuss any changes at least once a month, and twice a month we sync our calendars. We also discuss all major purchases, and come up with a game plan for making them.

In a nutshell, please know, ladies, this has nothing to do with gender. Household money management is a shared task with more responsibility leaning toward whoever is naturally better at handling the money. If you both suck at it, you're going to have to choose the person that sucks less, ensure you communicate openly, and keep a great team of financial professionals by your side. (See: *What professionals should I have on my financial team?*)

I CHOSE TO STAY HOME WITH THE KIDS. DO I STILL HAVE A RIGHT TO BE INVOLVED WITH THE MONEY MANAGEMENT?

Is this a trick question? Of course you do! As a member of the family, you're affected by the family finances and how any resources that flow into your home are managed. How your household income and expenses are handled will determine where and how you and your children live and what happens to your life once the children are grown and gone. It also determines what will happen to you in the event that you're faced with divorce or your husband's disability or demise.

Household money management is a shared task, no matter who earns the income. If you and your partner chose for you to stay home, there's real value associated with all the money saved in daycare and babysitting expenses, as well as the services you provide your family, so don't sell yourself short. No matter what, you each share the responsibility to manage your resources wisely. Don't give up your right to be involved, and definitely don't turn a blind eye to what's going on. If you choose to do so, you can't act like a victim when things don't end up the way you believe they should. (See: *How do we decide who should manage the money?*)

SHOULD COUPLES SHARE BANK ACCOUNTS?

Well, let's get the obvious out of the way. If you're not married, you definitely don't need to merge bank accounts or open a joint account. If you are married, I believe it's a matter of personal preference, but I heard a divorce attorney put it this way. "It's easier for a divorce if you keep your money separate, but it's better for a marriage if everything's in one pot."

When I coach couples occasionally, I recommend a His, Hers, and Ours bank account method. As suggested by the names, the couple creates one joint account that serves as a mutual money melting pot for household bills and other expenses, such as groceries and dry cleaning. This method may also extend to a second account, which houses joint savings for long-term goals like vacations, or home renovations.

While joint accounts may be a great test of your patience, they can foster transparency and build trust, as long as each spouse communicates and respects the agreed upon boundaries for use of those funds.

In the His and Hers accounts, each spouse basically gets predetermined fun money they can do anything with—no questions asked. If the husband wants to golf with his buddies, he should be able to do so free of judgment, as long as the household expenses are handled. The same goes for the wife. A night out with the girls or a pamper session at the local spa shouldn't become a blown out of proportion "discussion" simply because either party disagrees with how their spouse unwinds.

Joint accounts or not, there has to be open communication about what's going on. I teach my clients to treat the process like a business deal, free of emotions. If two companies merge, everyone has to start out on equal footing. Terms have to be agreed upon, and each partner should be fully aware of how accounts will be used.

DO YOU SUGGEST I KEEP A SECRET STASH MY PARTNER KNOWS NOTHING ABOUT?

I get asked this question more than you'd guess. While I completely understand the thinking behind it, and would be a complete liar if I said it hadn't crossed my mind in the early days of my relationship, it saddens me.

Hiding money, while encouraged by well-meaning mothers-in-law and protective daddies, is the bedrock of mistrust in a marriage. While it may feel like you have one up on the other person, you both lose when this secret stash eventually comes to light.

Hiding money doesn't help you solve the real problem at hand, which is that you either don't believe your husband is capable of sound money management or you don't believe the relationship will last. Both scenarios are embedded in deeper issues that don't disappear because you've got a few dollars tucked away.

Real MONEY

Agreeing with your partner to maintain minimum balances in your joint accounts can make you both more comfortable.

If you feel the urge to stash money, because you think your husband will spend every last penny of the family funds, then there are several other steps you need to take. As you learned earlier in this chapter, lack of communication is the top cause of divorce. In a non-threatening way, have a conversation about what financial thresholds make you comfortable and uncomfortable. For example, you may not like the checking or savings account to dip below a certain dollar amount. Explain this to him, and work together to come up with ways that you can both contribute to keep balances above the agreed upon minimum. If circumstances require a change to these standards, make sure the decision is reached mutually, so no one feels left out or guilty.

Realize that your mate had a certain way of doing things way before you came along. While you may believe that if he really cares about you he should, would, and could do what you want him to do, these things take time. I can honestly say it took at least three years for my husband and I to finally find a groove and create an our-way scenario, as opposed to the his-way and my-way methods we tried to force on each other in the beginning.

Real TALK

Secrets are secrets. You can't keep your own hidden stash of money and get mad at him for doing the same.

Ultimately, you're in charge of setting the boundaries you believe will protect you best. I can't define those for you, and neither can anyone else. I encourage you not to forget the Golden Rule: Do unto others as you would have them do unto you. Before you start keeping secrets in your relationship, understand that secrets are secrets. Don't justify yours and then condemn those he may want to keep, including his own hidden stash of money.

AT WHAT POINT SHOULD I ACCEPT THAT THE MONEY ISSUES HAVE COMPLETELY RUINED OUR MARRIAGE?

If your spouse honestly just doesn't get it, then you have some tough decisions to make. As a firm believer that there's hope in many situations, I'm pretty optimistic that with a bit of determination and teamwork, things will work out in your favor. But what happens when you've tried to improve communication, set boundaries, and shared what you know in a loving way, and things still aren't working out?

While my personal belief is that money should be managed collectively, in these extreme scenarios, you may decide to manage your funds separately. That means that while you may chip in on household bills like roommates, you'd be responsible for your own retirement, long-term care, and the like. Be aware, however, that this is a short-term fix. I've seen women who were diligent with their own financial affairs but stayed married to someone who wasn't. When the husband got older and became sickly, who do you think had to foot the bill?

Where my optimism fizzles, and I prefer to draw a line, is when your partner's mismanagement turns into blatant malice. If you two have debated so much about money that you now harbor resentment toward each other that manifests in nasty ways, it's time to reevaluate the relationship as a whole. If the mismanagement spirals into *intentionally* failing to take care of basic necessities, that's a problem. I've seen women exhaust retirement funds, abuse student loan refund checks, and land in tens of thousands of dollars in credit card debt because of their spouse's selfishness and the woman's desire to "keep the family together." Again, while I'm a strong proponent of marriage, I'm not tolerant of financial abuse.

My former pastor, Bishop Kenneth C. Ulmer of Faithful Central Bible Church in Inglewood, CA put it best when he said, "People should treat you how you want to be treated—not how they feel like treating you." If your gut tells you that you're being taken advantage of, please don't ignore your intuition because of me or what I've written here or what anyone else says. If you're just hurt and paranoid from a previous situation, that's one thing, but if you truly feel that you cannot trust your future or stability with a person, by all means follow your heart.

You're blessed with women's intuition for a reason. Sure, there are times that your wires may get a bit crossed, but the danger lies in failing to listen to your inner voice and allowing a man or a relationship to completely override your good judgment. If your instincts have you constantly concerned about what your mate will do financially and how it will impact you, embrace that feeling and address it. If it's a misunderstanding, then it should be easily resolved through counseling or by using the communication tips discussed throughout the section. If you're still concerned, you have some tough decisions to make.

HOW DO I RECOVER FINANCIALLY AFTER A DIVORCE OR BREAK UP?

Not only do women struggle to get back on track emotionally after a break up, they often find themselves fighting to recover financially. My desire to work with women in the area of personal finance stemmed from hearing about their trials during my early years as a broker. While there are a number of issues that may rise from a divorce, from stress to low self-esteem and depression, a lack of financial resources and ignorance of the concepts of how to manage money add insult to injury.

> **Real TALK**
>
> You'll never recondition what you don't recognize. Be honest with yourself.

Consider these steps as you work to heal both emotionally and financially.

1. **GET CLEAR ABOUT YOUR ROLE.** No matter what circumstances you face in life, good or bad, you have the primary role in deciding where you end up. Be honest with yourself. If you're in a financial mess, what did you do, or not do, that contributed to the matter? Did you participate in frivolous spending so the two of you could "live the life?" Did you acquiesce

when you knew you should have put your foot down? Were you okay with not knowing what was going on financially?

You'll never recondition what you don't first recognize. Once you acknowledge your part, you can figure out how to avoid the same type of destructive behavior in the future. The last thing you want to do is repeat the exact same pattern with a brand new person.

2. **GET EDUCATED ON WHERE YOU STAND FINANCIALLY.** Once you have a clear picture of how you ended up where you are, it's important not to let guilt get the best of you. Don't waste time beating yourself up. The real work to get your money right begins now.

Start by creating a budget based on your new solo income. Depending solely on yourself means you'll need to implement some discipline to get things in order. (See: *How do I know if I've created a realistic budget?*) Next, pull your credit report at www.annualcredit-report.com. Make sure everything you see is actually something you recognize as your debt. If your ex has any fraudulent activity going on, you're going to need to address it ASAP. (See: *What should I do if there are items on my credit report I don't recognize?*) If it's all yours, add it up, and create your plan for debt elimination. (See: *What is a debt eliminator, and how do I determine my debt-free date?*)

3. **GET PROFESSIONAL HELP.** Look into no-cost or low-cost consumer credit counseling in your area by visiting the National Foundation for Credit Counseling at www.nfcc.org. You want to find a counselor that can help you set realistic financial goals and get a sound plan in place to meet your unique needs at this delicate stage of life.

FRIENDS & FAMILY OR FINANCIAL FOES

HOW DID WE GET here, ladies? I understand that we tend to be caretakers and givers by nature, and that's fine. But where did we learn that we need to be responsible for and take care of *everybody* from adult children to the church itself? What has allowed us to overdo it to the point that when we have an emergency and need something for ourselves, we're depleted? We have nothing left to give emotionally or financially.

The inability to have much needed conversations about money extends well beyond the romantic realm. I don't know very many people who haven't been asked to loan a loved one money or to take on some financial responsibility for a friend or family member at some point. From picking up the tab for a girlfriend who's not working, but still insists on going out every weekend, to covering a payment for your first cousin who keeps forgetting rent is due at the same time every month, you've likely been faced with, or will be faced with, the decision to financially aid someone close to you. While you may find this noble, if you're not careful, it can eventually affect you negatively. You can give to the point you have nothing left to meet your own basic needs. And if you're riddled with debt and don't have adequate savings, you're on a slippery slope that can potentially leave you broke, no matter how well you attempt to manage your finances.

There are many instances in which you may believe you're helping, and every once in a while, perhaps you are. But when you allow another grown

I deserve and enjoy the finer things in life.

individual to become a line item on your struggling monthly budget, you have to ask yourself who you're really helping and who you're hurting. As singer, actor, and author, Tyrese Gibson once shared in a discussion, "Sometimes to help someone, you have to stop helping them." Learn to empower, not enable. Don't turn friends and family into financial foes.

HOW CAN I TELL IF I'M FINANCIALLY ENABLING SOMEONE?

If there's even a thought in your mind that you might be enabling someone, then you probably are. But to be 100% clear, an enabler is one that

"Sometimes, to help someone, you have to stop helping them."

enables another to achieve an end; especially one who enables another to persist in self-destructive behavior (such as substance abuse) by providing excuses or by making it possible to avoid the consequences of such behavior.

Before you move on feeling some sense of superiority, please note that while the definition cites substance abuse as a self-destructive behavior, it doesn't disqualify those that financially enable friends and family. It's one thing to assist someone who finds himself or herself in a bind from time to time, but it's another to add their needs to your monthly expenses. Not only is this form of helping them actually hurting them, but it can be hurting you, as well.

Listen, I know how it feels to think you're obligated to assist family and friends. After all, isn't it the noble thing to do? It might be, if it weren't for the fact that this kind of nobility can often create an inability in people to figure it out on their own. Financially speaking, "it" can be a number of things from how to earn their own income and manage their own money wisely to how to distinguish between their wants and needs, how to hustle, and how to pay their bills on time.

So how can you tell if you're enabling someone in your life? Answer yes or no to the following questions.

Do you:

1. Constantly find yourself having to bail out grown and able-bodied adults? (If you're a parent and your "baby" is above college-age, yes, they count as an adult.)

2. Tell the few people who actually offer to pay you back not to worry about it?

3. Financially support anyone whose neediness is purely derived out of their own laziness?

4. Find yourself afraid for this person, or convinced that he/she can't handle basic life situations without falling apart?

5. Excuse this person's behavior as a result of the economy, stress, misunderstanding, or difficulty coping, even when the behavior hurts or inconveniences you?

6. Feel like you have a unique and special relationship with this person, unlike anyone else they may know?

7. Feel protective of this person, even though he/she is an adult and is capable of taking care of his/her life?

8. Wish others in this person's life would change their behavior or attitudes to make things easier for this person?

9. Feel reluctant to refer an individual to a source of help or assistance, because you doubt that anyone else can understand the situation the way you do?

10. Ever feel manipulated by this person but ignore your feelings?

11. Make yourself available to another person at the expense of your own financial obligations, energy, or time?

12. Hear from others that you're too close to this person or the situation?

If you thought "yes," committed a shy nod, bit your lower lip, or rested your chin in the palm of your hand and leaned forward, then more than likely you, my friend, are an enabler.

Real TALK

Real need inspires real motivation.

So without further ado, here's how you can stop enabling those you claim to love.

1. **STOP ENABLING AND START EMPOWERING.** There's an old, yet relevant Chinese proverb which says, "Give a man a fish, and you'll feed him for a day, but if you teach a man to fish, you'll feed him for a lifetime."

   Don't take away a person's ability to hustle. The fact of the matter is that you won't always be around to go fishing for them. If you keep enabling them, they'll starve once they have to go it on their own. Do you really want to leave someone you care about without basic money survival skills?

   Remember, *real need inspires real motivation.* People will not learn to be responsible as long as they know they'll always have you as a backup plan.

2. **INSTEAD OF REACHING IN YOUR WALLET, REFER THOSE IN NEED TO COMMUNITY RESOURCES AND SERVICES.** Your constant helping tells them, "I support your self-destructive and negative behavior so much I'm going to give you more money, so you can keep it going."

   Actions speak louder than words. You can give the inspirational "get your life together" speeches all day, you can get angry and swear before the Almighty that this is the last time you'll help, until the cows come home, but what you *do* is always speaking so much more loudly than what you *say.*

3. **TAKE *YOU* OUT OF THEIR PROBLEMS.** This is not about *you* being an awesome person. This is not about *you* doing your good deed so you can make it through those pearly gates. In fact, this isn't about *you* at all. This is about each person figuring out life on her own.

   If nothing else, remember that the money you continue to dole out to irresponsible friends and family members could be used to get yourself out of debt, buy your first home, or save for your retirement. There's nothing selfish about considering yourself every once in a while. After all, the folks you're enabling definitely don't care about you or your future, and believe me, when your money runs out and you have nothing else to give, they'll just move on to the next overly generous enabler.

HOW DOES CO-SIGNING A LOAN FOR SOMEONE ELSE AFFECT ME?

When you co-sign for a loan, you basically tell the lender that you accept equal responsibility for the loan's repayment. You're guaranteeing that if the borrower fails to pay, you'll make the payment! You're not just helping your friend or family member get a loan. You're literally promising that you'll pay the debt yourself if the borrower doesn't. Studies have shown that as many as three out of four co-signers (75%) ultimately end up making payments on the loan.

When you co-sign, you're promising to pay the debt if the borrower doesn't.

So what happens if you co-sign on a loan and the borrower defaults?

1. If the lender decides to sue and actually wins, your wages can be garnished or liens and judgments can be placed against your personal property until the debt is satisfied.

2. Your credit report can be severely tarnished from several months of late payments, as well as a judgment against you.

75% of co-signers ultimately end up making loan payments.

3. You may eventually have to pay up to the full amount of the debt, in addition to late fees or collection costs.

If for some reason none of the above scares you, and you're still considering co-signing for a friend or relative, please *always* remember these tips.

1. **KNOW THE PERSON YOU'RE ATTEMPTING TO HELP.** Before agreeing to sign on the dotted line, study the person's financial habits and make sure you're comfortable with his or her money management skills.

2. **VERIFY THAT PERSON'S EMPLOYMENT AND TAKE HOME PAY BY REVIEWING PAYCHECK STUBS AND BANK STATEMENTS.** If the borrower doesn't want to share that type of personal information, he shouldn't be asking you to put your credit-worthiness in jeopardy.

3. **UNDERSTAND YOUR OWN CAPABILITY.** Make sure you have enough income left over each month to pay the minimum payment on this account should something occur unexpectedly.

4. **BE SURE YOU HAVE AN OPPORTUNITY TO DISCUSS ALL OF THE TERMS OF THE AGREEMENT WITH THE LENDER.** This is your loan just as much as it is the borrower's. Know all the details of what you're getting into.

If you feel uncertain about one or more of the above points, seriously reconsider co-signing. Think about the reason this person can't qualify for a loan on their own. There's good cause for why the bank isn't willing to take on that risk. If she damaged her own credit, don't be fooled into thinking she'll take better precautions to protect yours. Protecting your credit is up to you!

SHOULD I LEND MONEY TO FRIENDS?

Never lend money that you can't afford to give. Loaning money to your friends, or even family, is a really bad decision when you're not truly in a position to do so. If you want to lend money to someone in need, you may as well as consider it a gift and let go of any expectation that you'll get the money back. If they repay you, great! If they don't, then there should be no love lost, because your primary concern was helping them out, and you did that.

Real MONEY
Never lend money you can't afford to give away.

The problem with some folks is that they'll keep coming back once they realize how generous you are. During college, I was mentored by author and comedian Steve Harvey, who always says, "The best thing you can do for a poor person is *not* become one of them." I wholeheartedly agree. Learn now to say *no*, and teach your friends and family members how to do just what you're learning how to do—take *personal* responsibility for their *personal* finances.

If you decide to lend money to someone, at least take a few precautionary steps to help protect your interests.

1. Be clear about what the money is for, and be sure there are no alternatives you can help the borrower come up with before you reach into your own pocket.

2. Put the terms in writing, so all parties involved understand that this is a loan and not a gift.

3. Set up a repayment plan with a firm due date. Either agree to accept a realistic number of equal installments or determine a date when all funds should be made payable. Outline the consequences for non-payment.

4. If possible, make sure the agreement is made with someone else present as a witness.

5. Always leave a paper trail. Exchange funds via money order, cashier's check, or personal check. Never give cash.

6. Please reconsider, and don't lend money!

Seem cumbersome? Great! It's designed to. My hope is that you require so much, the person wanting to borrow money would rather take their sob stories and broken promises elsewhere.

WHAT'S WRONG WITH BORROWING MONEY FROM MY FRIENDS OR RELATIVES EVERY ONCE IN A WHILE?

Unless we're talking about borrowing $25 or less until you can find your misplaced debit card, you absolutely should not be borrowing money from people. I'm not really a fan of lending money, but I'm even less of a fan of borrowing. What your friends and family probably don't have the heart to tell you is that they see you as "that person." Yes, you're the one they avoid at all costs, because they know borrowing money is a way of life for you. What they don't want to tell you is they wish you'd get it together and stop treating them as if they're your personal ATM, or even worse, as if their opportunity fund is your opportunity fund. Is that clear enough? Good. Tell them to thank me later.

Listen, I'm not trying to "shame you to death," as my granny would say, but someone has to tell you. Unless we're dealing with extremely unique and unusual circumstances, you shouldn't borrow money, especially if you don't earn a consistent income and can't commit to a solid plan for repayment. Do you think your friends and family members can honestly afford to just give you money? I know you said "borrow," but if they lend to you, more than likely they'll end up having to accept that they gave you the money, or you'll lose the relationship all together.

Don't put your loved ones in an awkward position. Borrowing money makes relationships tricky. If you're truly in a bind and your friend loans you money, the first time she see you with something that even remotely looks new, she'll think to herself, "She owes me money, but she has new shoes on?" I say, just avoid this altogether. Don't borrow from people who genuinely mean something to you, and if, despite everything I've said, you feel you have to ask to borrow money, don't be mad when folks turn you down.

HOW DO I DEAL WITH GIRLFRIENDS WHO HAVE IT ALL?

I'd love to tell you that the majority of the women I've counseled and coached over the years wound up buried in mounds of debt primarily because of student loans or unexpected medical expenses. Too bad I can't. Much of the debt my clients find themselves in comes from buying stuff they really didn't need in the first place, like shoes, purses, jewelry, home improvements, and expensive cars. When we work toward getting to the root of why they make purchases they don't need and can't afford, those that are honest typically mention a close girlfriend, family member, or neighbor who had something the client wanted.

Remember the saying "birds of a feather flock together?" It's natural to be attracted to things that a friend might have, but that doesn't mean you should try to keep up with her lifestyle, especially when she's in a totally different tax bracket. It's more than possible to maintain a wonderful friendship, and remain understanding and respectful of each other's circumstances.

Use these strategies to deal with friends that may not share your financial struggles.

1. **DON'T TRY TO KEEP UP!** Just because your friends can shop every weekend, doesn't mean you should attempt to do the same. Be realistic about what you can spend, otherwise you'll run yourself into debt trying to figure out how to keep up with someone who may be doing this effortlessly, or who may be worse off than you are, despite her Oscar-worthy performance as a rich girl.

2. **DON'T MAKE THEM FEEL GUILTY.** If you see your friends spending what you believe is "too much money," don't chastise them or attempt to make them feel guilty. It'll make you appear bitter about your own circumstances. If you genuinely want to share personal finance tips and advice with them, do it in a helpful and supportive way, and teach by example.

3. **MAKE SUGGESTIONS THAT WORK FOR YOU.** If your friends aren't bound by the same budgetary constraints you are, they may suggest you bond over shopping at the mall or dining in some pricey café week after week. Even if you don't want to go into tons of details about your own situation, don't be afraid to suggest alternative hang-out options. You can search for the best cheap eats in your town, or get your friends to check out the cool new thrift store you discovered.

4. **RETURN THE FAVOR ON YOUR TERMS.** If your wealthier friends start to pick up on the fact that your wallet is a little lighter than theirs, they may want to treat you more when you go out. It's normal to want to reciprocate, but you'll obviously have to figure out ways to return the favour within your means. Offer to have a low-key dinner at your place one Friday night, or find other creative but inexpensive ways to hold up your end of the friendship.

5. **USE ANY NEGATIVE FEELINGS FOR GOOD.** Understand that any feelings of jealousy you may experience are completely normal. Find a way to make those emotions work for you. Use them to motivate you to accomplish your own financial goals as quickly as possible. Turn the pain into a greater purpose.

Most importantly, never forget to keep things in perspective. You never know what financial situation a person may truly be in. Many people appear to have it all, but you have no idea what they may be going through to keep up appearances.

I THINK MY FRIENDS ARE TAKING ADVANTAGE OF ME FINANCIALLY. HOW DO I PROTECT MYSELF, BUT KEEP THE FRIENDSHIPS?

I hate to be the one to break this to you, but if there are people taking advantage of you financially, or in any other manner, they're really not your friends. By the time you've gotten to the point of asking this question, you're aware of who your real friends are.

If you have friends you believe genuinely care about you, but they still expect you to help them out financially because they think you can, try making them aware of the problem. Tell your friends you're feeling used. Ask them plainly if they're only hanging around you because of your ability to pay for things, or is it because they truly enjoy your company.

Understand there are two parties in this type of co-dependent relationship: the used and the user. You're allowing yourself to be used. Think about why you would continue to befriend a person who only wants to take advantage of you. Are you otherwise lonely? Is it hard for you to make friends for some reason?

A few years ago, I coached a client named Erin. She made good money as an in-home care provider, but could never smoothly meet her monthly obligations. After just three sessions, we realized that all of Erin's money was being lent out to friends who never paid her back, many of them repeat offenders. So why would she keep letting them take advantage of her? She was buying their friendships. Erin didn't have many friends growing up, because she was known as the class nerd. Back then, she made a few friends by buying lunch for people. At thirty-two years old, she was doing the exact same thing with much bigger numbers and to her own financial detriment.

You have to uncover and acknowledge the root of this problem, and it doesn't begin with the friend. It begins with understanding your own value as an individual. Erin didn't need to buy her friendships, and neither do you.

To find out whether or not these people are genuinely interested in friendships with you, take money out of the equation. Don't lend anyone money or offer to purchase anything for them. Keep conversations pertaining to money to a minimum, or eliminate them altogether. Take note of your friends' reactions when you have no money to offer, and see how long they stick around. Those that still show up and continue to invest in your relationship are actual friends. The others don't deserve your friendship, and you should be more discriminating in who you choose to call "friend" in the future.

HOW DO I FIND THE COURAGE TO SAY *NO* TO A LOVED ONE THAT NEEDS HELP?

It's amazing that *no*, only two letters, seems to be the hardest word for many of us, especially women, to say out loud. Strangely, it seems easier to say, "Of course, I can!" or "No problem!" or "I'll be glad to!" Even as you agree, you know you don't want to do whatever it is, and furthermore, you can't afford to do it.

In order to say *no* to requests that will negatively affect your finances, you have to relearn how to say *no* with the same enthusiasm as the average two-year-old. People-pleasing is a learned behavior. After plenty of spankings and redirections from adults, we finally give in and drop *no* from our vocabulary. Instead, we substitute lots of ways to be agreeable and keep other people happy, even to our own detriment.

$ Real MONEY

To protect your money, relearn how to say "no" with the enthusiasm of a two-year-old.

You know which of your friends and family members seem to find themselves in sticky situations because of the poor choices they continue to make, and you know who's dealing with an unfortunate circumstance beyond their control. Deep down, you also know which of those people will never get it together. At least they won't as long as you continue to intervene.

In the *Mindset + Money Master Class*®, I remind participants often that we're each blessed with unique gifts, talents, and skills we can use to produce financial gain. Those gifts are given to us freely, but it's our responsibility to choose whether or not we'll cultivate and use them. When we don't, we typically suffer unnecessarily, not just in our finances, but emotionally and spiritually, as well. When you continuously rescue people from the consequences of their own behavior, you handicap them. You become an obstacle on the journey to uncovering the God-given gifts that

could change their lives and their destinies. In all your efforts to help, you hurt them in a way that will have lasting effects.

Stop looking at it as saying *no* to their requests. See it as your chance to encourage them to say *yes* to the bigger blessings for their lives. The same source which sustains you can sustain them, but only if you'll get out of the way.

I SAID *NO*, AND NOW MY LOVED ONE ISN'T SPEAKING TO ME. WHAT NEXT?

First let me tell you what's *not* next: giving in again. When you finally get the courage to say *no* to a repeat offender, embrace the fact that for once

I am surrounded by loving, loyal, and solid relationships.

you chose your personal finances over someone else's. Recognize that you deserve to make your desire to save money, pay off debt, and send your own children to college debt-free the highest priorities for the money you work hard to earn. Don't be guilted into feeling anything negative about putting your own needs and wants before someone else's need and want to borrow your money.

Some people will only come into your life for a reason or a season. Whether you're dealing with a close friend or a beloved family member, sometimes you have to embrace the gift of goodbye. Not everyone will travel with you to the next phase of your financial transformation. Being in your life is a privilege, and you have to regard it as such. Not everyone deserves that privilege, especially those that choose to be angry with you because you're finally ready to make your dreams a reality.

I know this may seem harsh, but leaving someone behind doesn't have to mean you never speak to them again, unless they're truly toxic. It does mean, however, that you now define for yourself if and how you'll allow them to utilize your time, energy, and resources.

It's time to ask yourself a critical question: ***Where are the ships in my life taking me?***

Ships are designed to take people places. If your relation(ship) or friend(ship) isn't taking you anywhere, but is constantly taking away from you, it may be time to abandon ship.

KIDS & MONEY

WHILE MOST OF US can agree that financial education ought to be a mandatory class in every high school, college, and university just as much as biology, algebra, or any other core class, we've yet to see this happen. Until we wake up as a nation and take a united stance to make it so, teaching our kids about money is still up to us, ladies. Despite knowing this, it's been reported that parents are still more likely to talk with their kids about manners, grades, eating habits, drugs and alcohol, and the risks of smoking than about managing money wisely.

The New Living Translation of Proverbs 19:18 says "Discipline your children while there is hope. If you don't, you will ruin their lives." Whether your child is two years old or thirty-two years old, you're still playing a very important role in how they interact with money. At any stage, you have the power to handicap them for life or to help them harness a strong sense of financial stability.

Instilling financial discipline is easiest at a young age, especially if you can do it in an engaging and practical way that will make wealthy habits come naturally. Maybe your "little ones" are fully grown adults, and you've spent the majority of their lives enabling them. Don't worry. As long as there's still breath in your body, it's not too late to turn it around.

If your children are still minors, remember those little cuties won't be kids forever. If you want to break some generational curses and cycles, you've got some tough decisions to make. And you better make them quickly, because your kids and your money are both depending on you.

HOW CAN I MAKE SURE MY YOUNG CHILDREN HAVE FUN LEARNING ABOUT MONEY?

Teaching children about money doesn't have to be difficult. Younger children are so eager to learn all they can and be more adult-like that they're willing to try anything once, especially if it's interesting. I find the clients that have the most problems sharing financial concepts with their children struggle because they're battling their own issues with money. In order to really help your children, you've got to get over any fear of not being perfect with money and remember you definitely know more than enough to meet a ten-year-old's needs.

$ Real MONEY

The best way to encourage conscientious spending habits in your children is to exhibit those habits every day.

Here are a few to ideas get you started.

1. USE CASH WHEN POSSIBLE.

There's no minimum age on being a smart saver and conscious spender, but showing younger kids how to budget and spend through the use of a credit or debit card won't do much good. More often than not it's too abstract for a young mind. A child is more likely to equate a card with an endless supply of resources on the other end. Kids need to see money, and see it leaving your hand in exchange for something else, as much as possible. This teaches them that most things in life come at a cost and when the money is gone, it's really gone. Start with something as simple as allowing small children to deposit coins in a parking meter or occasionally paying for your purchases in cash.

While younger children may understandably have trouble grasping the concept of off-site savings, they have no problem with piggy banks for their coins and a wallet for dollars. As soon as they're old enough to count, encourage them to periodically add up their money and see how much they've saved. The physical action of putting the money back in the piggy bank or wallet will teach them that they don't have to spend every dollar they have and that saving is encouraged and absolutely normal. As their savings grow, you want to remind them of what they had at last count and what they have now. Don't forget to continuously praise them for being great savers.

2. USE PRACTICAL, EVERYDAY SCENARIOS.

The best way to encourage conscientious spending habits is to exhibit them in everyday life. When planning a trip to the grocery store, get small children involved in making the list. Make sticking to it a game. They're likely to ask for something extra. Your goal is to teach them to avoid a would-be saver's biggest obstacle: impulse buying. Tell them the dollar amount you wish to spend (your budget) upfront and make hitting the number or coming in below it a high-five moment at the checkout stand.

You can also help little ones set goals early. Start with small things like books or small toys that cost less than $10. Challenge them to do extra tasks around the house to earn money, so they can buy the item on their own. When they reach their goal, congratulate them and encourage them to set an even larger goal. Help them search online for an item they'd like to buy that costs around $25. The goal is to teach them patience and planning. The sooner your child learns delayed gratification, the better. Print out a picture of the item that includes the price, so they can keep it in a safe place near their piggy bank or wallet. When they're tempted to do something else with their money, this will serve as a great reminder of their goal.

For more worthy and ambitious long-term goals, you may want to consider matching grants. For example, you can offer to give them $1 for every $5 they save toward the purchase. This will reward your child's savings discipline.

3. USE BOTH PHYSICAL AND DIGITAL GAMES.

Don't forget old school board games the family can play together. You might be surprised by how today's versions have been modernized. Take Monopoly for instance. According to the description of Monopoly's Electronic Banking edition, "It's all about flash, not cash." Players use bank cards instead of paper money. Take a look at my favorite, The Game of Life. The 2007 Twists & Turns version uses a Visa Game Card instead of cash and allows you to determine how many years you'll play before determining who's become most successful after assessing assets and liabilities.

Fortunately, with today's technology, there are many ways to make learning about money fun for kids of all ages. The Internet is full of age-specific money games for kids. Start by checking your financial institution's website. Many banks and credit unions have created fun videos and games to teach kids about money. They make the topic of money entertaining for kids, and they can be used to create an open and interesting family discussion. They also provide backup for what you're already teaching, so you're not always the one preaching about money. You can look for money games on a number of trusted sites online, like www.pbs.org and www.kids.usa.gov.

WHEN AND HOW DO I GIVE MY CHILDREN AN ALLOWANCE?

According to the online resource *Kids Money*, the average parent who pays their child an allowance begins when the child is around seven years old.

Real TALK

Children should earn money, just as adults do.

Most money experts agree that children should be *given* an allowance in order to learn financial skills. I disagree. Children should *earn* money, just as we do. Either way, the conversations you—the parent—have about what to do with the money are essential to ensuring your children become fiscally responsible.

Why do I believe your kids should earn the money? A majority of the students I meet as I speak around the country understand that they're in college to become productive citizens who earn a living. Unfortunately, many of them have no idea how the whole process works. Why? Because they've been *given* money their entire lives for things they should technically do anyway, like be respectful, clean their bedrooms, empty the trash, and earn good grades. On top of all that, they receive annual raises for simply getting older. When's the last time you got a raise for keeping a tidy office, showing up to work on time, or having a birthday? Just checking.

Here's the deal with paying your kids for meeting their basic obligations. Once they have other streams of income, like a part-time job or birthday money from grandma, they'll draw a blank when you expect them to do chores at home. Why should they clean up for you when they just got free money for doing nothing? Instead, they need to know basic household chores are just their contribution to the family. It goes like this:

I feed you. You do the dishes.
I drive you to school. You wash my car.
You walk around my house. You vacuum.
You asked for a little brother or sister. I gave you one. Now, you babysit.

See where I'm going with this?

Now, any task over and beyond basic household chores is where the earning potential comes into the picture. As parents we take on the burden of having to get so many things done in any given week. What can your kids help with? Need someone to file papers? Do you need a closet or drawer organized? Get creative. We know kids need money, but how can you teach them a valuable lesson and get both party's needs met?

A major downfall of this entire allowance thing is that many parents implement an allowance with no expectation for how the child should manage the money. In the real world, we don't earn a paycheck and still have the luxury of someone else paying our household bills and covering all of our necessities. That was the point of earning the money.

Parents are responsible for the basics, but kids who earn money should become responsible for the frills. Let me tell you how my mom did it. We'd discuss upfront how much she believed something should cost. If what I wanted went over that amount, I was responsible for the balance *and* the taxes! Talk about lessons that last a lifetime. After a few embarrassments at checkout registers, this method quickly taught me how fast money could go when I was buying things just to keep up with the Joneses. After every trip to the mall, my mom was fine. She spent only what she wanted to spend. Nothing more. No hard feelings—on her part, at least.

Maybe your children have cell phones on your plan. You want them to be able to call you in case of an emergency, but they should be required to earn the money to pay for the extras, such as texting and accessories. That's not for you! It's to stay in constant touch with their friends. If your children are of driving age, teach them the responsibilities of driving by having them pay for gas every other week or by requiring them to contribute money for auto insurance. My mom added me to her gas card, but I was responsible for the bill from the time I was a senior in high school until I was a senior in college and had to get my own card. Think that helped me cut down on my generous offers to give every friend a ride? Yes, it did.

The important thing to realize here is that allowance is fine, but it needs to come with conditions. You're not going to traumatize your kids by teaching them how to be responsible with money. What are you protecting them from? Real life? They need to know the importance of living beneath their means, giving, and saving. If we wait until they're leaving for college to get the conversation started, we're missing an essential part of the job of preparing them for adulthood.

I THINK I MAY HAVE ENTITLED CHILDREN. CAN THIS BE CHANGED?

As parents, we want to see our children grow up with more opportunities and access than we may have had. That's understandable. What's not

Real TALK

Children learn to be responsible or entitled according to which attitude you reward!

understandable, however, is raising children who believe they're due something in life simply because they're breathing. Being responsible, understanding the value of money, and expecting that privileges are to be earned rather than given, are all character traits far too difficult to teach with words, or we'd all memorize a few magical phrases and have perfect children.

Answer the following questions to determine whether what you're sensing in your child is a true sense of entitlement.

1. WHAT HAVE YOU BEEN REWARDING?

We learn to be responsible or entitled according to which attitude is rewarded. To teach responsibility, accomplished behavior must be rewarded. To teach entitlement, something other than accomplished behavior is rewarded. Training a child to be entitled is a very easy task. As parents, we do it constantly by rewarding children for merely existing. We don't require that they demonstrate consistent behavior before we give privileges. While it may be permissible, it's not beneficial to give more money just because the child has reached a certain age. That type of thinking assumes that a child will automatically demonstrate responsible behavior as a result of growing older. Often the expectation that the child act responsibly is lost, and the only requirements for reward are being born and having another birthday.

2. HAVE YOU USED YOUR CHILD TO DISPLAY YOUR OWN LEVEL OF SUCCESS?

Some parents do this by giving their children privileges earlier than their stage of development warrants. Ever see a five-year-old in the mall with a cell phone? Or the fourteen-year-old who can't drive, but gets a brand new BMW for her birthday? Could you expect a child with these types of privileges to *not* feel entitled? What could a child in either scenario honestly do to deserve these extravagant and age-inappropriate gifts? The answer is nothing. Please note these are not rewards. They are unearned privileges. This is about the parent wanting to look or feel rich, not about what's actually in the best interest of the child's long-term growth and maturity.

3. ARE YOU MOST CONCERNED WITH YOUR CHILD'S HAPPINESS?

If your main goal in parenting has been to make the world a perfect, pleasant, and extremely happy place for the child at all costs, then you must acknowledge the role you've played in creating this false sense of entitlement. Wanting your kids to have things easier than you did, can lead to what's known as the "entitlement model of parenting."

4. DO THE FOLLOWING BELIEFS RESONATE WITH YOU?

a) Children deserve and have the right to be happy all the time.

b) Parents need to protect their child from experiencing natural consequences that result from irresponsible behavior. For example, it's okay to lift a restriction and allow the child to attend a practice, so he or she can play in the game on Saturday.

c) The only way to judge a child's responsibility level is to listen to what the child says or promises he or she will do in the future.

d) When children reach a particular age, they have rights to certain privileges. If they demonstrate incompetence after the right is given, the right can be taken away and the child will understand that he or she should now work for what previously was given for nothing.

If you agreed with any of those statements, you should know that what you teach an entitled child is that they should be rewarded for existing. This leads them to the following conclusions.

Real TALK

It's your duty to teach your child responsibility.

- *My life should consist of the pursuit of happiness, pleasure, and fun.*
- *You owe me what I need to have a pleasant, fun life.*

- *I can and should be angry when I'm asked to do something to earn what I believe is owed to me.*
- *I can and should be angry when privileges are taken away, because they belong to me.*

With beliefs like those, the entitled child is usually lazy and often belligerent. They don't feel it's necessary to plan ahead or consider others when making plans. An entitled child has no understanding of the fact that their own behavior can result in positive or negative consequences. The entitled child often says things like: *everybody else is doing it, it's their fault, that's not fair, I need,* and most often, *I want.*

Sound familiar?

I hope not, but if it does, understand that if your child isn't learning what you want him or her to learn, it's up to you to change that. It's your duty to teach them responsibility.

A responsible person is defined as one who understands that there are consequences for behavior and therefore plans ahead, so the consequences will be pleasant rather than unpleasant. As a parent, you can only judge the child's mastery of responsibility by evaluating the child's behavior. To teach responsibility requires you to reward a child for accomplished tasks, rather than for expected behavior or future plans and promises. You have to teach children that their own behavior defines their lives. Continuous responsible behavior brings positive rewards, including financial freedom and freedom in any other area of life. Continued irresponsible behavior results in rewards not being given in the first place and may result in their temporary loss when mistakes are made.

For a different result, you must become dedicated to teaching your child that they don't automatically get things just because they exist. As a result, he or she learns to respect and appreciate others' efforts, because they have a personal understanding of what it means to earn something. In addition, you want them to develop a personal sense of empowerment and self-esteem, because they know that their own behavior will determine what they get in life.

Children learn to be responsible or entitled over time, depending on which behavior their parents reward. To unlearn either model will also take time. If your child is consistently disrespectful, despite your efforts at parenting, and you find yourself feeling helpless or incompetent in this area, the child has likely developed an attitude of entitlement. To change this you'll have to change your beliefs as a parent, start rewarding your child only after consistently demonstrated positive behavior, and be willing to tolerate your child's unhappiness in the meantime.

YOU REALLY THINK KIDS SHOULD WORK?

Are you serious? You probably don't want to ask the woman who's been working unofficially since she was six years old and illegally since she was thirteen. By first grade, my mom would take me with her and farm me out to other departments in the hotel she worked in to do everything from stuff envelopes to organize and alphabetize folders in junky file cabinets. By seventh grade, I spent every holiday and vacation from school at another hotel working in the Human Resources department. I did everything from answer phones to data entry, and by sixteen years old, I had my own office where I screened applicants, completed background checks, and trained newly hired employees. So again, do you really want to ask me this question?

Real TALK

You really don't understand the true value of money until you've earned it yourself.

My grandmother used to say, "You really don't understand the true value of money until you have earned it yourself." By encouraging kids to work, parents can effectively teach their children the value of money and help them understand that money really doesn't grow on trees. It's unfortunate, but in this day and age, you'll find college students who aren't sure where money comes from. Remember our chat about entitled children? (See: *I think I may have entitled children. Can this be changed?*)

Allowing your kids to work isn't going to kill them. In my opinion, it'll probably save them. For starters, we live in a competitive society now. Your children are no longer competing against the neighborhood kids in their class. They're dealing with global competition in a marketplace in which whoever can get the job done efficiently and effectively can have it, no matter where they live in the world! If the best a young adult has to offer is the same education most of their peers got, how competitive are they? Work experience, understanding hierarchy and corporate culture, the confidence of knowing how to interact with adults, and the like will set those young people that work apart from those that don't. And at the end of the day, employers don't have time to help your children mature. They expect you to have already done that.

Here are a few work ideas for kids at different ages:

YOUNG KIDS: Younger children may not actually work in the traditional sense, but they can take on simple tasks around the home and garden to earn a little income. My five-year-old shreds paper in my home office or dusts windowsills throughout our home to earn money. When children get a little older, they can find odd jobs around the neighborhood, like mowing lawns, shoveling snow, or raking leaves to earn a few extra bucks.

PRE-TEENS: During the pre-teen years, your children can earn their own cash by baby-sitting, pet-sitting, or tutoring other kids. This is a good time to teach them a little about entrepreneurship. Have them assess their gifts, talents, and likes to see if they could be the solution to any problems in the neighborhood.

TEENAGERS: Once your children reach the teenage years and show some financial maturity, you should encourage them to get part-time jobs. Teenagers can find work at supermarkets, restaurants, department stores, and other local businesses around your neighborhood. You'll ideally want something in walking distance, so they aren't stressing you about needing a car.

The opportunity to get a job needs to be accompanied by some rules. Not only should you help your teenager predetermine how earnings should be divvied up, so he or she understands your expectation for savings, you should also set other ground rules. Before agreeing to a particular job, discuss work hours, schoolwork commitments, expectations for grades, and household responsibilities with your teen.

WHAT SHOULD I BE DOING TO MAKE SURE MY CHILD CAN ATTEND COLLEGE DEBT-FREE?

In its most recent survey of college pricing, the College Board reports that a "moderate" college budget for an in-state public college during the 2012–2013 academic year averaged $22,261. A moderate budget at a private college averaged $43,289. Now consider an additional independent 2012 study reporting 53% of recent college graduates are either unemployed or working as sales clerks, waiters, janitors, and other positions that don't require a college degree. While that's not what you want to hear as a parent, it's a reality you have to face. These are sobering statistics that should make you think twice about borrowing money for your kids to go to college, especially if you haven't saved at all or have under-saved for your own retirement.

UN REAL

In 2012, 53% of recent college graduates were unemployed or working in jobs that don't require a college degree.

Taking on a boatload of debt so your children don't have to be saddled with it isn't a good plan, but there are ways you can prepare for your children to go to college debt-free. You may be surprised to hear, however, that only a small portion of this plan will actually include you. Most of the work will be up to your children. Begin thinking less about what you have to do and more about how you'll teach them the importance of what *they* have to do.

For your part, one of the best things you can do is to save in a vehicle that's specifically set up for college expenses. If you think putting money aside in a regular savings account is going to do the trick, you should probably think again.

Look into a 529 plan. It's an account designed to encourage families to save for educational costs. It's almost like a 401k, except it's geared solely toward college expenses. A 529 comes in two forms: pre-paid and college savings.

The pre-paid plan allows you to purchase tuition credits in your state's university system at current tuition rates, which protects you against hikes in tuition. The potential downside is that your child may not get into a state school or may not be interested in attending one. In that case, you can withdraw the money and pay penalties or transfer the plan to another child.

The college savings plan is a tax-advantaged account that allows you to accumulate assets to use toward any accredited college or vocational school in the United States. The funds can be used to pay for expenses like tuition costs, textbooks, and other education-related fees.

Real MONEY

It takes years of deliberate planning to create a debt-free strategy for attending college.

Now, this going to college debt-free stuff is pretty much out of your hands from here. Of course, you can harass and nag your kids, their teachers, and school administrators to death, but this works out so much better when you instill these two guiding principles in your child.

1. College is expensive.

2. You probably won't go unless you do your part.

Harsh? Yes. But for many, it's the reality, and they shouldn't be protected from the truth. It's not the kind of surprise anyone wants to get during the application process. It takes years of deliberate planning to create a debt-free strategy for attending college. Even the parents who dedicate their lives to little league sports to try to snag athletic scholarships understand that. Similarly, those of us with children who may not be athletically inclined need to put the same energy into creating a "scholarship brand" for our children as early as possible. Jessica Johnson, the founder of The Scholarship Academy, a non-profit organization that helps families create and perfect their scholarship brand, says children as young as second grade can begin not only creating their brand, but applying for scholarships.

The most important thing, Johnson says, is figuring out the child's likes and strengths and then making sure everything from extracurricular activities to volunteer opportunities support the same themes. Your child can look like an expert by eighteen and become a real asset to the right college program.

While The Scholarship Academy and programs like it focus on helping young people with average grades succeed in landing scholarships, a major factor in helping your kids go to college debt-free is encouraging them to keep their grades up, which is also ultimately their responsibility. Being awarded free money is really a numbers game. The better the student's grades are, the more opportunities he or she has to earn money neither of you will ever have to repay.

Some people are discouraged because of the smaller dollar amounts that many grants or scholarships offer, however it's important to realize that every dollar counts and can add up quickly. Any amount you don't have to borrow is an even larger amount you won't have to stress about paying back in the future. Seek out a resource at your child's school to help you navigate the financial aid process, and check out sites like www.scholarships.com.

The goal is to get your child in place for two types of free money: grants and scholarships. Both can be used to fund a college education debt-free. Unlike with loans, the recipients aren't required to repay the money upon graduation or at any point in the future. While both scholarships and grants allow students to pay tuition without incurring debt, there are a number of key differences between the two. (See: *What's the real difference between grants and scholarships?*)

Grants and scholarships should be the primary forms of payment for college education, and loans should be an absolute last resort. Most importantly, the majority of the financial aid work must be done by your child. Of course, you understand the importance of attending college debt-free, but that won't mean a hill of beans if they don't understand it, too.

HOW CAN I SAY *NO* TO MY ADULT CHILD?

Turning down the financial requests of others might be a cinch, but how the heck do you say *no* when it's your child? Many parents don't talk to young children about money because of the fear that the children will be burdened with adult worries before their time. There are two holes in that theory. First, children won't fear something they fully understand. Education begets empowerment; ignorance does not. Second, little kids become big kids very quickly, and big kids become adults in the blink of an eye. If you miss this very short window of opportunity to teach your child the meaning of the word *no*, it's likely you'll have to continuously face these types of issues with your grown son or daughter.

AFFIRM

I empower others to create their own wealth and power.

The most important thing in these scenarios is to realize that while you may still see your cute little baby when you look at this person, this is your adult child—with the operative word being "adult." This is an able-bodied person that you're both enabling and handicapping. This is a talented and gifted adult that you're hurting, not helping. Contrary to what you believe, your child can and will figure it out when you're not there to save her or him from the trials every adult may experience at some point in life.

Think about it. Have you experienced certain setbacks? Did you live to tell the story? Well, they will, too. Some of life's greatest lessons are learned through experience. To appreciate the high moments in life, you have to know what the low points feel like. If you constantly shield your adult children from having to find a way back from those low points, you not only rob them of the satisfaction of knowing they can make it on their own, you block their chances at success and continuously make yourself out as the answer to all their problems. Once you're gone, they're left defenseless in the real world, which isn't what you want for them. Your goal should be to guide and empower them while they have you here.

The bottom line is to truly help someone, even your own child, you sometimes have to stop helping them. (See: *How do I find the courage to say "no" to a loved one that needs help?*)

APPENDIX A
PRINT RESOURCES

THE FOLLOWING BOOKS MAY prove to be excellent resources for developing further knowledge around what you have learned in Real Money Answers for Every Woman. My hope is that by browsing through the resources below you will ultimately find the style that works best for you. Your journey cannot stop with Real Money Answers. This book is a tool to assist you with becoming aware about how to make healthy financial decisions. Additional resources will ensure that you maintain them as you move through your money journey and quest for financial freedom. Enjoy!

APPENDIX B
SAMPLE LETTERS

CREDIT REPORT DISPUTE LETTER

Debt B. Gone
123 Your Home Address
Your Town, GA 01234

The Credit Bureau
Bureau Address
Anytown, ST 56789

Date

Dear Credit Bureau,

This letter is a formal complaint that you are reporting inaccurate credit information. I am very distressed that you have included the below information in my credit profile due to its damaging effects on my good credit standing. As you are aware, credit reporting laws ensure that bureaus report only accurate credit information. No doubt the inclusion of this inaccurate information is a mistake on either your or the reporting creditor's part. Because of the mistakes on my credit report, I have been wrongfully denied credit recently for a <insert credit type for which you were denied here>, which was highly embarrassing and has negatively impacted my lifestyle. The following information therefore needs to be verified and deleted from the report as soon as possible: CREDITOR AGENCY, acct. 123-34567-ABC Please delete the above information as quickly as possible.

Sincerely,
Signature
Printed Name
SSN# 123-45-6789

Attachment included.

(Don't forget to provide proof if you have it! Keep a copy for your files and send the letter registered mail.)

* Remember this can also be done online by visiting the credit bureaus website.

DISPUTE LETTER TO INDIVIDUAL CREDITOR

Date
Company name
Address

Re: Acct # XXXX-XXXX-XXXX-XXXX

Dear CEO name,

I am writing to you today regarding my credit card account #4236-XXXX-XXXX-XXXX which I had while I was a student at --------------------------. The purpose of my correspondence is to see if you would be willing to make a "goodwill" adjustment on the reporting of this account to the three credit agencies.

During the time period this account was established I had was very happy with the service, I was however not the ideal customer and made mistakes with my handling of the account. I should have kept better records regarding the account and I take full responsibility. I became aware of the unpaid balance when I got a copy of my credit report in _____ of 20____.

I know that payment was my responsibility. I am not attempting to justify this breach of my user agreement. I was, however, hoping you might review the circumstances under which this non-payment occurred and consider removing the negative trade line from my credit reports.

As soon as I became aware of the balance I contacted ---------------- and paid the balance in full. I provide this not to justify why the account was unpaid, but rather to show that the issue with ----------- is not a good indicator of my actual credit worthiness. I hope that ---------------- is willing to work with me on erasing this mark from my credit reports.

I would like to STRESS that the information currently being reported IS accurate, (I am not disputing anything with ---------------). I am simply asking -------------for a courtesy gesture of goodwill in having the credit bureaus remove this account from my report. I do recognize that this request is unique and that it may not be ------------ normal policy. Please consider that the Fair Credit Reporting Act does not demand that all accounts be reported, only that any account that is reported be reported accurately. Therefore, a company does have legal discretion and permission to remove any account it chooses from the credit report. I'm hoping that ------------ will do that in my case for this account.

Your kind consideration in this matter is greatly appreciated.

Best Regards
Signature
Printed Name

LETTER TO HARASSING CREDITOR

Sally B. Struggle
123 Your Home Address
Your Home Town, CA 01234

Harassing Creditor
Creditor Address
Anytown, ST 56789

RE: Account Number

Date

Dear Harassing Creditor,

To whom it may concern:

Please be advised that on the following dates, _____, I requested that your representative _____ stop calling me at home or at work. These continuous calls are serving no purpose but to harass me. I realize that I have a financial obligation to your company. However, my present financial situation makes it impossible for me to meet our original terms.
I am exercising my right granted by the Bureau of Consumer Protection, a division of the Federal
Trade Commission, to request that no one from your company call me at home or at work again.

If you must contact me, please do it via U.S. Postal Service.

Thank you in advance for your cooperation.

Sincerely,
Signature
Printed Name

APPENDIX C
ASSORTED WORKSHEETS

CREATING A PERSONAL FINANCIAL PLAN

These questions are the foundation for creating a personal financial plan.

1. Assessment: *Where are you now*? Use numbers and dollar amounts to be specific about where you are with respect to savings, debt and any other financial data you want to start tracking.

_____

_____

_____

_____

_____

2. Goal Setting: *Where do you want to be?* Again use specific terms to define where you would like to be financially by a set time at some point in the near future.

_____

_____

_____

_____

_____

3. Creating a Plan: *How will you get there?* Do you need to stop spending or get a job in order to reach your goals? List three things you can begin doing within the next 30 days to get you on track.

_____

_____

_____

_____

_____

4. Execution: *Taking action and making it happen.* There's no time like the present to take action on creating the life you say you want! List an action you can start in the next 24 hours.

_____

_____

_____

_____

_____

5. Re-Assessment: *Repeating the process regularly.* Determine in advance how often throughout the year you will check in on your progress and re-assess if necessary. I would suggest at least every six months.

_____

_____

_____

_____

_____

SAMPLE MONTHLY BUDGET

Of course your expenses and therefore, budget, will vary based on your personal lifestyle habits, but this is a great place to begin to list the numbers you'll need to work with. Remember, it doesn't matter which budget you use – you just need to use something!

PATRICE C. WASHINGTON
Author | Speaker | Coach

MONTHLY PROSPERITY PLAN

Monthly Income		Monthly Expenses	
Your Pay	$	Rent or Mortgage	$
Spouse's Pay	$	Utilities (Phone, gas, electric, cable, etc.)	$
Bonuses	$	Insurance (home, auto, life, health, etc.)	$
Commissions	$	Food	$
Tips	$	Incidental Home (non-food items, etc.)	$
Interest Received	$	Clothing	$
Investment Earnings	$	Auto (car note, gas, maintenance)	$
Rental Income	$	Debt Payments (credit cards, store cards, etc.)	$
Pension Income	$	Child Care	$
Social Security Income	$	Health (medical, dental, eye, etc./not covered)	$
Alimony Received	$	Taxes (not taken out of paycheck)	$
Child Support Received	$	Gifts (charities, church)	$
Other Income	$	Entertainment (movies, vacation, videos, etc.)	$
	$	Personal Allowances	$
	$	Other Expenses	$
	$		$
Totals	$		$

MEET PATRICE C. WASHINGTON

Patrice C. Washington has been making money educational yet fun since 2003. She is a featured columnist, television commentator, radio host, author, speaker and leading authority on personal finance, entrepreneurship and success for women and youth.

Patrice's wisdom on money matters has been featured by national brands including:

NBC	**The Huffington Post**	**GEICO Now Magazine**
Upscale Magazine	**HelloBeautiful.com**	**Experian**
Bankrate.com	**BlackEnterprise.com**	**Madam Noire**

Each year, conference coordinators, churches and colleges nationally have trusted Patrice to entertain, empower and educate thousands on personal finance, business and success. Patrice doesn't bore audiences with financial jargon and fluff they can't use. She selflessly tells the story of her own journey and unlike many is not ashamed to share both her triumphs and her setbacks. After personally writing over 300 articles for print and online media, Patrice's brain is jam-packed with practical tips anyone can take and implement immediately.

When Patrice isn't making audiences laugh and learn somewhere around the country, she's at home in Atlanta, GA being entertained by her fun-loving daughter, Reagan and extremely supportive husband, Gerald.

For more about Patrice, visit www.BookTheMoneyMaven.com.